FORTRESS BUDAPEST
II.

Kamen Nevenkin

FORTRESS BUDAPEST[2]

The siege of the Hungarian capital, 1944-45

© PeKo Publishing Kft.

Published by
PeKo Publishing Kft.
8360 Keszthely, Bessenyei György utca 37., Hungary
Email: info@pekobooks.com
www.pekobooks.com

Author
Kamen Nevenkin
© Kamen Nevenkin, 2020

Photos
TsAMO, Strategia KM, Fortepan, Magyar Nemzeti Múzeum, Hadtörténeti Intézet és
Múzeum, Mirko Bayerl, Pawel Sembrat, Kamen Nevenkin, Krisztián Ungváry

Printed by
Gyomai Kner Nyomda Zrt. in Hungary
www.gyomaikner.hu

First published
2020

ISBN
978-615-80072-5-2
978-615-5583-31-5

All rights reserved. No parts of this publication may be reproduced,
or transmitted in any form or by any means, electronic or mechanical,
including photocopying, recording or by any information storage
and retrieval system, without permission from the Publisher in writing.

Table of contents

Maps 7

Strongholds 25

Sketches 189

Photos 225

Leaflets 461

FORTRESS BUDAPEST
MAPS

MAPS

List of keys

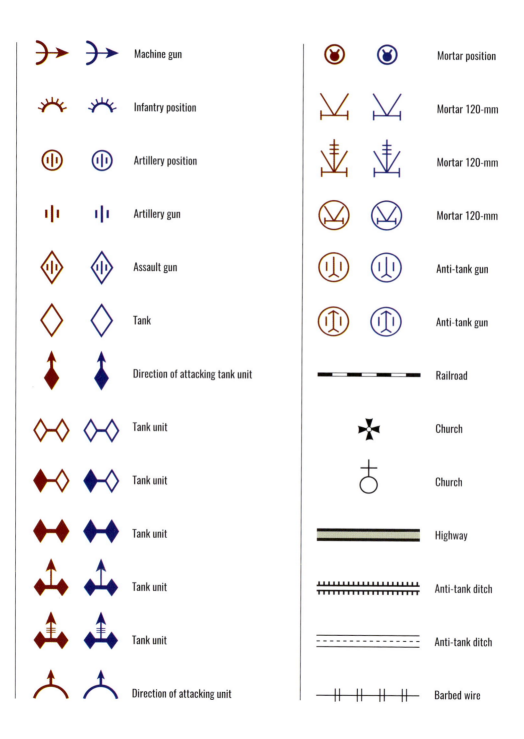

List of abbreviations

AAAR = Anti-Aircraft Artillery Regiment

AD = Advance Detachment

AFV = Armoured Fighting Vehicle

APC = Armoured Personnel Carrier

Arm. = Armoured

ATAR = Anti-Tank Artillery Regiment

CD = Cavalry Division

Div. = Division

GA = Guards Army

GABD = Guards Airborne Division

GAMR = Guards Artillery Mortar Regiment

GCC = Guards Cavalry Corps

GCD = Guards Cavalry Division

GCR = Guards Cavalry Regiment

GFR = Guards Fortified Region

GHSPAR = Guards Heavy Self-Propelled Artillery Regiment

GMC = Guards Mechanized Corps

GMcBn = Guards Motorcycle Battalion

GMorBn = Guards Mortar Battalion

GMRBn = Guards Motorized Rifle Battalion

GMRBr = Guards Motorized Rifle Brigade

GRC = Guards Rifle Corps

GRD = Guards Rifle Division

GTA = Guards Tank Army

GTBr = Guards Tank Brigade

GTR = Guards Tank Regiment

GTBn = Guards Tank Battalion

HAR = Howitzer Artillery Regiment

Hus. = Hussar (Hungarian)

Inf. = Infantry (Hungarian and German)

Kav. = Cavalry (German)

LAR = Light Artillery Regiment

McBn = Motorcycle Battalion

MGABn = Machine gun Artillery Battalion

MIBr = Marine Infantry Brigade

MorR = Mortar Regiment

MRBr = Motorized Rifle Brigade

MRBn = Motorized Rifle Battalion

MRCoy = Motorized Rifle Company

OP = Observation post

Pz. = Panzer (German)

RBn = Rifle Battalion

RCoy = Rifle Company

RC = Rifle Corps

RD = Rifle Division

RR = Rifle Regiment

SPABr = Self-Propelled Artillery Brigade

SPAR = Self-Propelled Artillery Regiment

SPG = Self-Propelled Gun

TBr = Tank Brigade

TC = Tank Corps

MAPS

Capture of Budapest

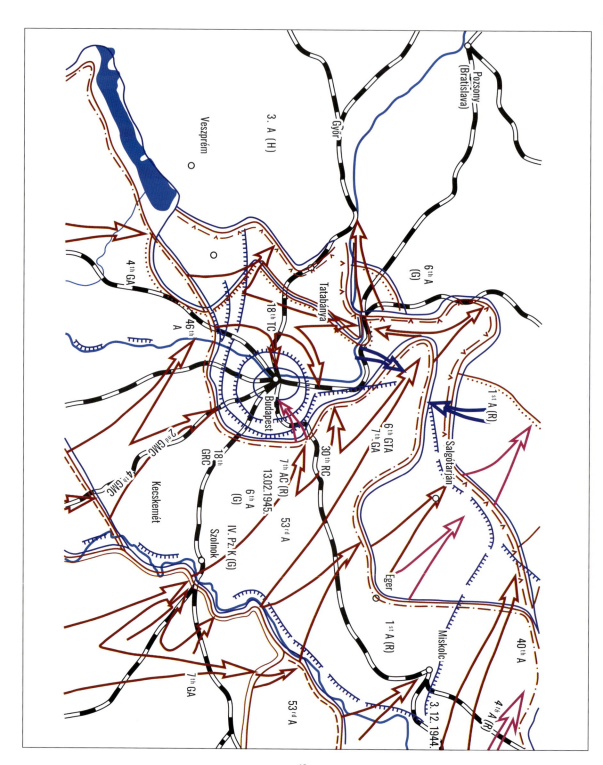

Fortress Budapest

The Defence of Dunaharaszti around 3 November 1944

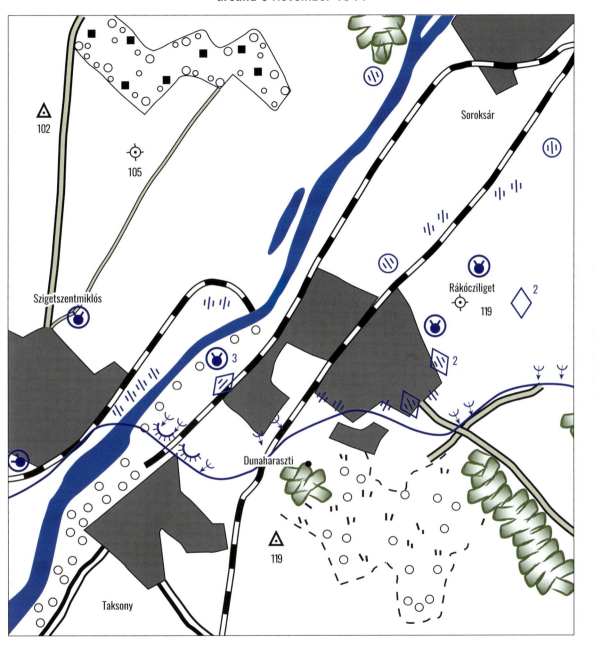

MAPS

Attack of 15th Guards Mechanized Brigade and 202nd Guards Rifle Regiment towards Dunaharaszti on 3 November 1944

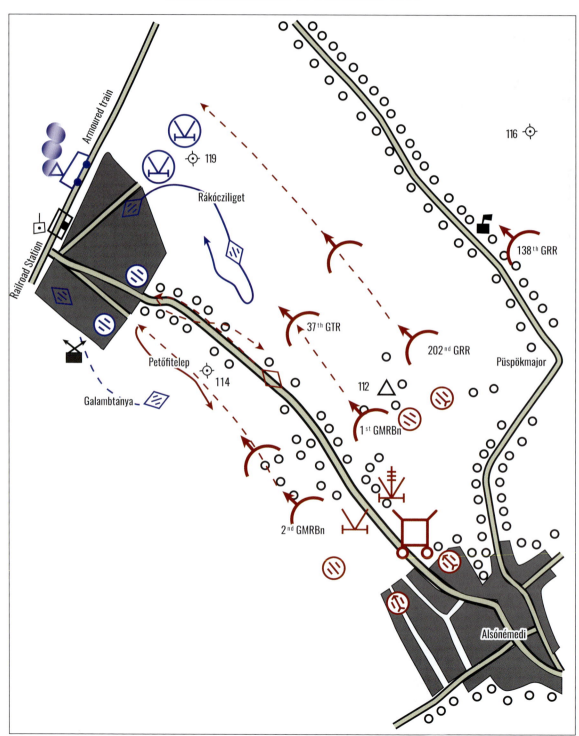

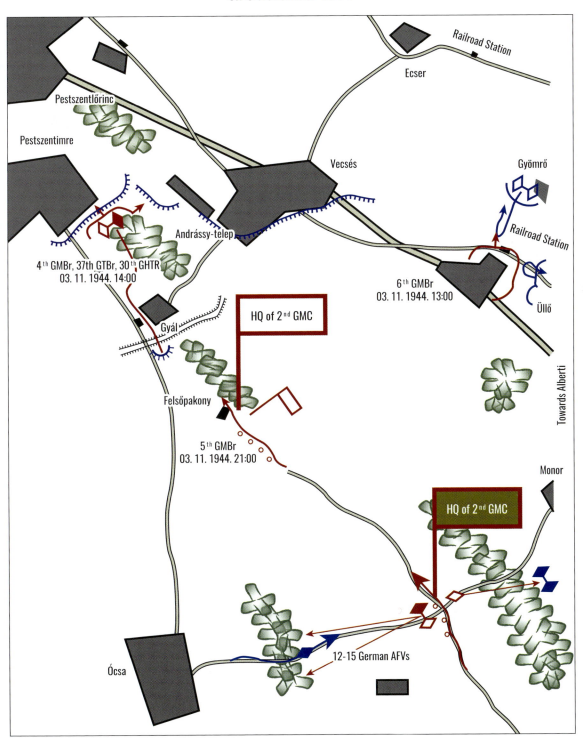

MAPS

Combat Actions of 2nd Guards Mechanized Corps on 4 November 1944

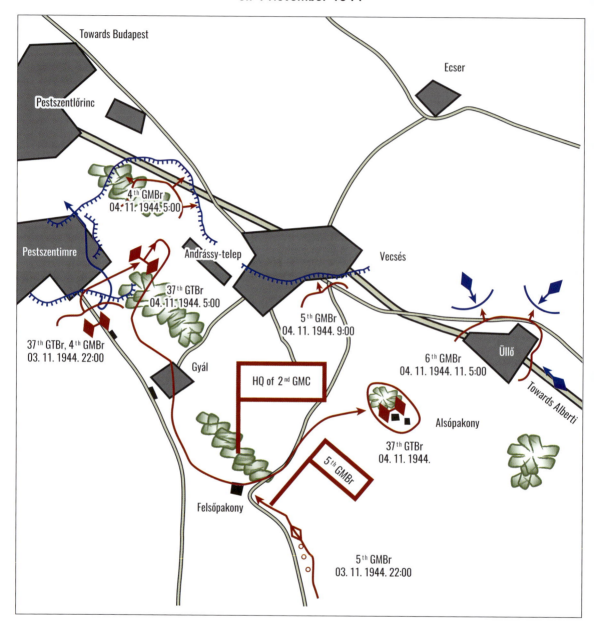

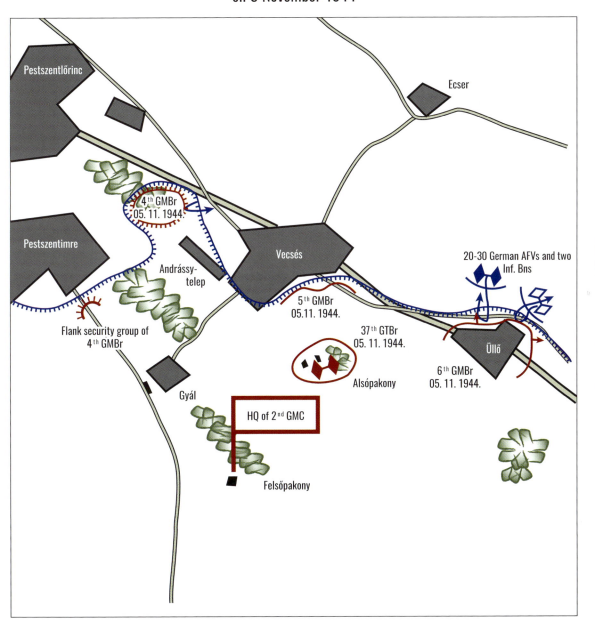

MAPS

The Attack Plan of 109th Guards Rifle Division on 3 December 1944

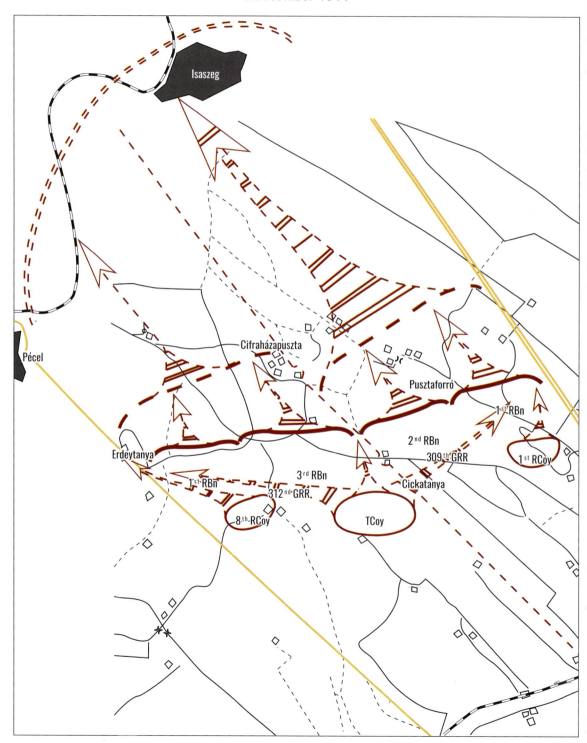

Attack of 5th Guards Tank Corps near Dunakeszi

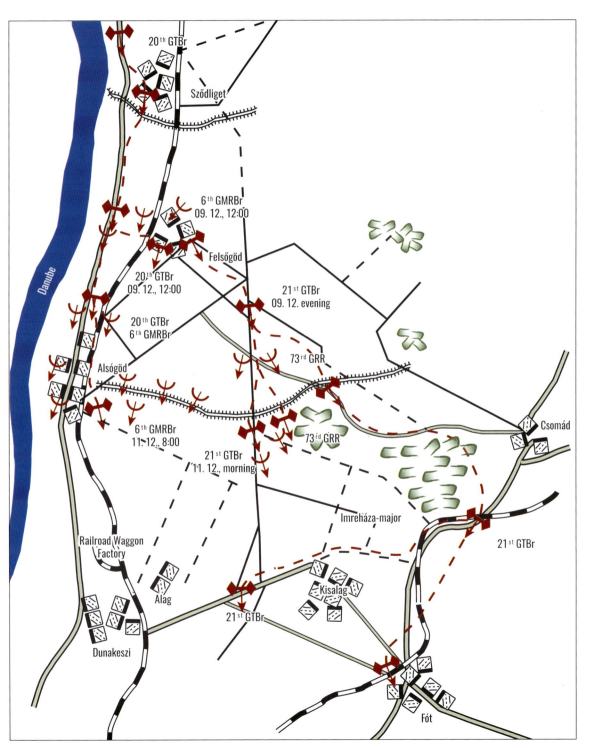

MAPS

The Soviet 5th Guards Tank Corps near Vác

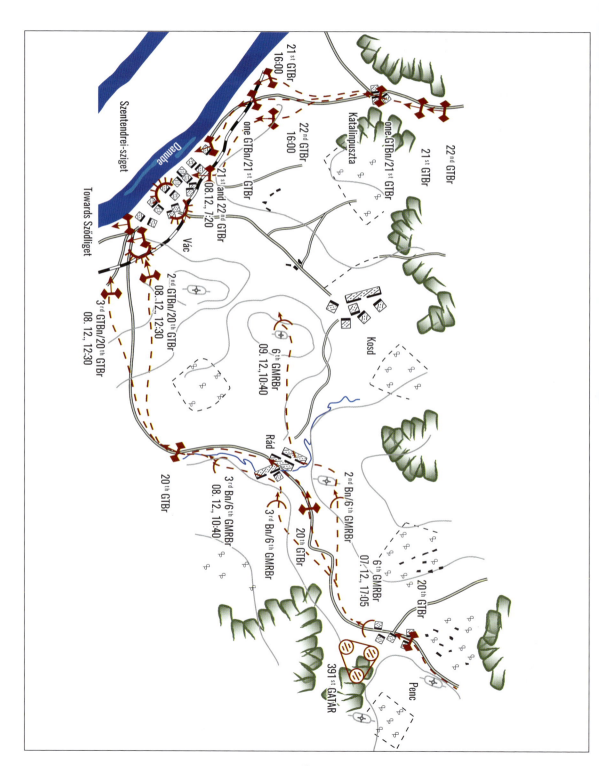

Attack of Soviet 30th Rifle Corps against northern edge of Pest

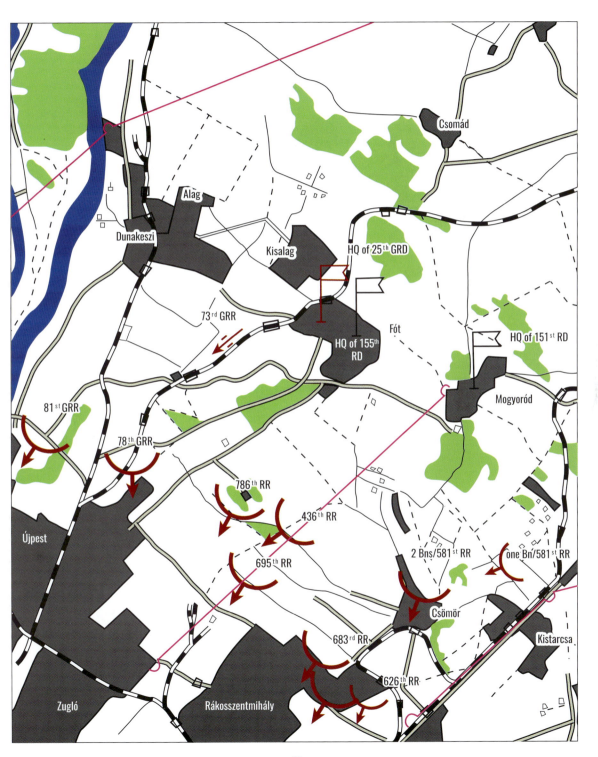

MAPS

Combat actions of Soviet 27th Guards Tank Brigade between Galgamácsa and Őrszentmiklós

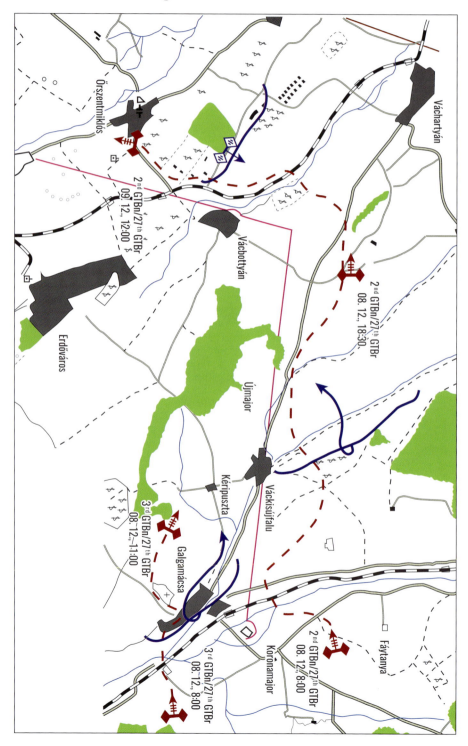

Fortress Budapest

Combat actions of Soviet 27th Guards Tank Brigade near Csomád

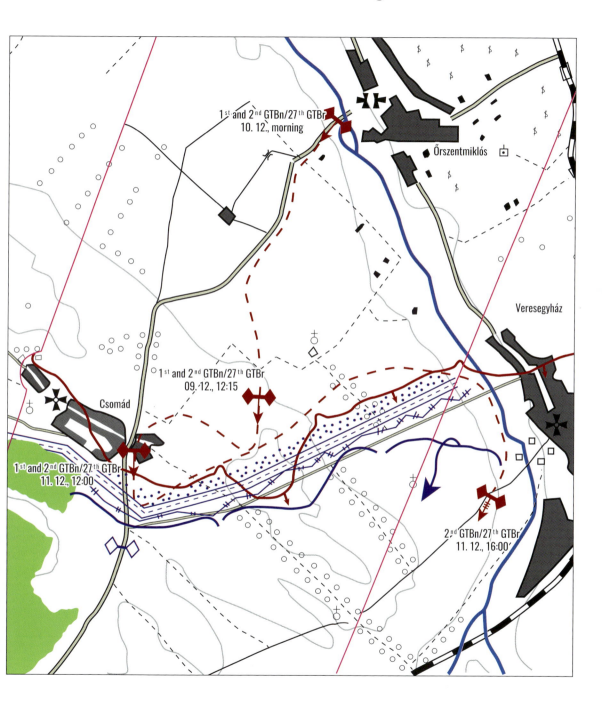

MAPS

Combat actions of Soviet 27th Guards Tank Brigade near Mogyoród

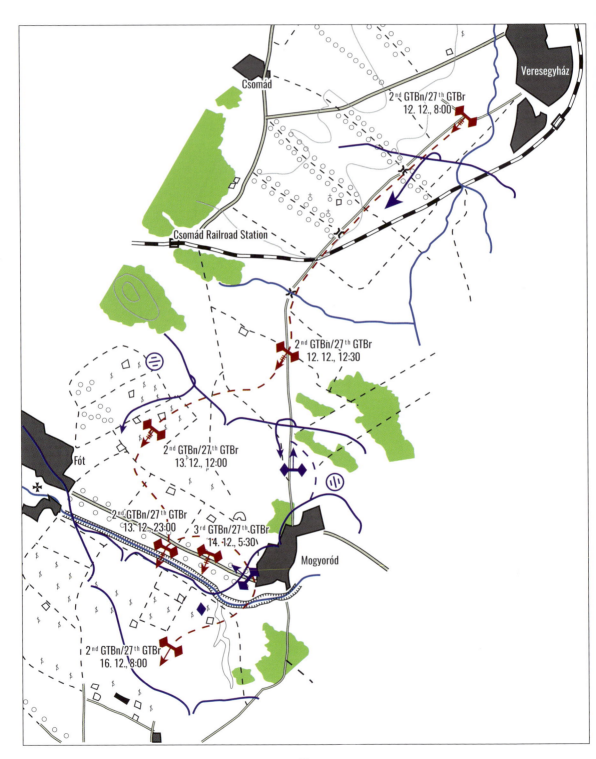

Combat Actions of Soviet 11th Guards Cavalry Division against the German-Hungarian forces after breakout from Budapest northeast of Buda, 12-17 February 1945

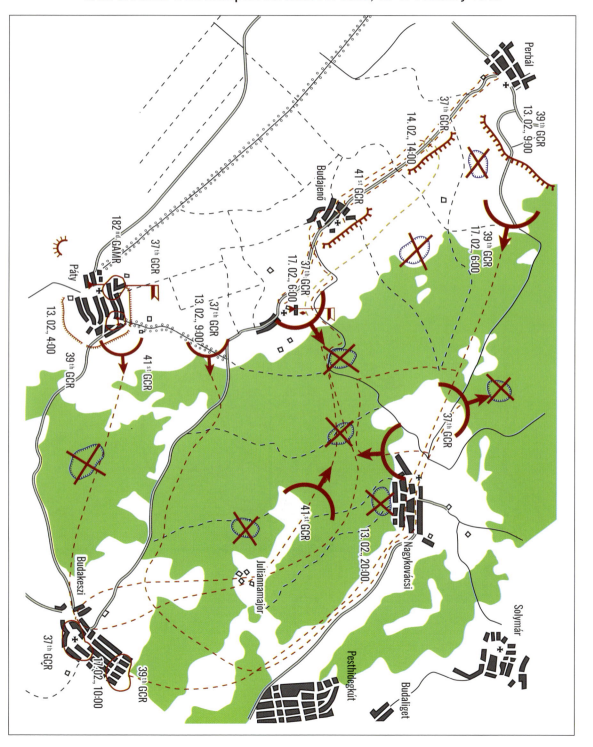

MAPS

Deployment of 3rd Ukrainian Front units against the German-Hungarian elements after breakout from Budapest, 12-14 February 1945

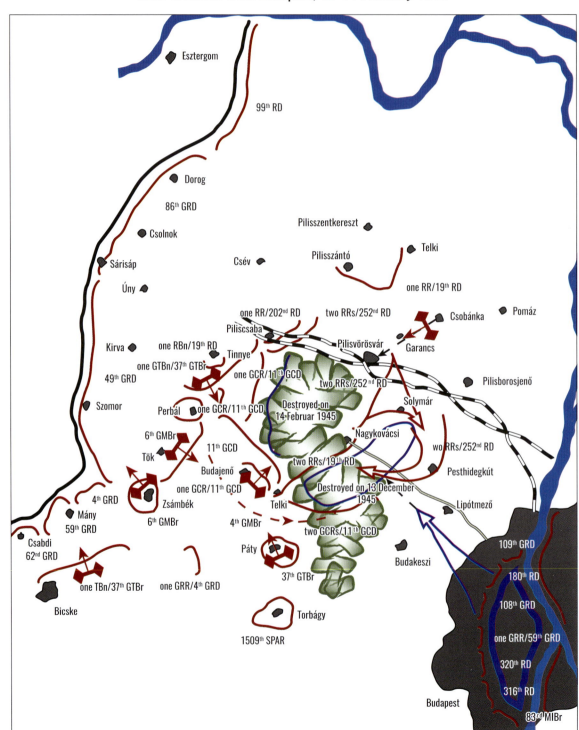

STRONGHOLDS

FORTRESS BUDAPEST

STRONGHOLD 1

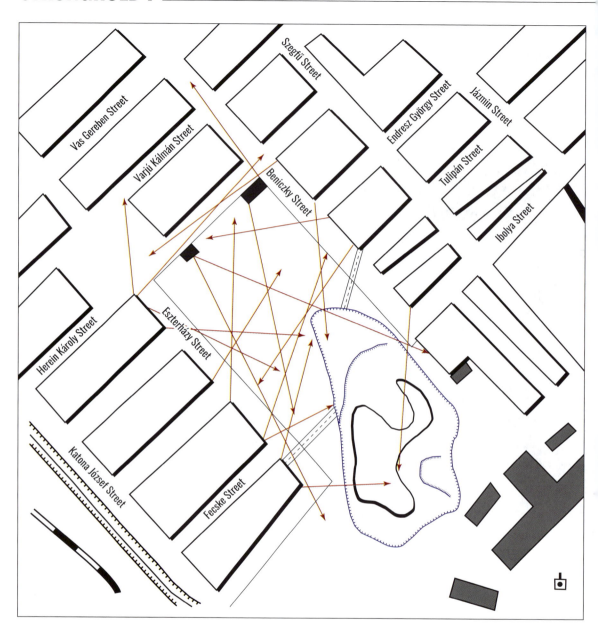

Kispest consisted mainly of one-storey buildings and was not suitable for a long-term defence. In an attempt to strengthen that sector, the defenders had dug-out an anti-tank ditch with a triangular cross section that was about 2.5 metres deep and 4.5 metres wide. The stone houses were used as firing positions.

Captured Hungarian and German tanks.

Anti-tank ditch

A single-storey house turned into a bunker.

Captured Axis guns

An artillery position behind a stone fence

STRONGHOLD 2

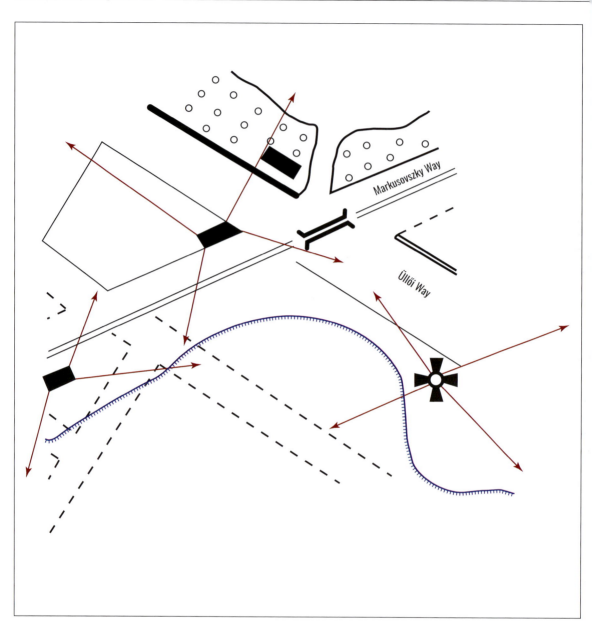

Direction of fire

Trench

Church steeple

Üllői Way was one of the main thoroughfares of Pest. In the outer part of the city it was integrated into the existing defensive system by fortifying the residental buildings and digging out trenches. In the inner part of the city the buildings were also integrated into the main defensive line, but were not especially fortified. The wide, open space to the south of Markusovszky Way offered good possibilities for the defenders.

The wide open space to the south of Üllői Way.

Ferenc József Infantry Barracks and the open space in front of it.

Üllői Way in the inner part of the city, where the Soviets encoutered no fortified buildings.

The Holy Cross Parish Church was surrounded by trenches and turned into a strongpoint.

STRONGHOLD 3

The stronghold protected the southeastern approaches to Kőbánya. There were two lines of trenches (dug out some 100-150 m from the buildings) and an anti-tank ditch.

The outskirts of the stronghold were defined by a trench line.

A view on the stronghold.

STRONGHOLD 4

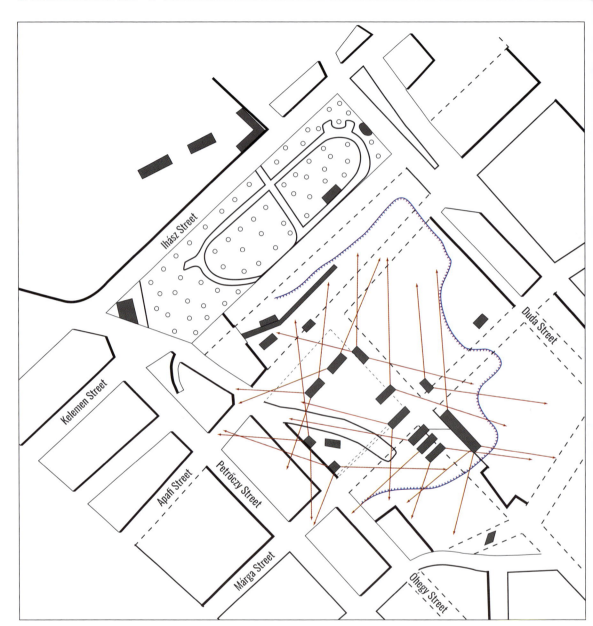

Direction of fire

Trench

Fortress Budapest | Strongholds

This stronghold was situated in the middle of Kőbánya. It was made up of several large and tall buildings, a water tower, a fire station with a tower, and the buildings of a brewery.

A view of the square in front of the water tower.

Water tower.

Fire station with a tower.

STRONGHOLD 5

The stronghold was situated on the northeastern limits of Kőbánya. In front of it there was a clear, open space that was 1.5 km wide. The nucleus of the stronghold was the building complex of the brickworks and several residential houses. It controlled the Budapest - Jászberény motorway.

A view of the building housing the masonry oven.

A residential building integrated into the stronghold.

A view of the masonry oven.

STRONGHOLD 6

Direction of fire

Railroad

Fortress Budapest | Strongholds

The stronghold was situated on the northern limits of Kőbánya, at the intersection of Kolozsvári and Maláta Streets. In front of it there was a clear open space that was 1.5 km wide. It controlled the northern approaches to Kőbánya. The nucleus of the stronghold was the building complex of the brewery and several stone residential buildings.

This five-storey stone residental building was integrated into the stronghold.

A close view of the brewery.

A view of the brewery.

STRONGHOLD 7

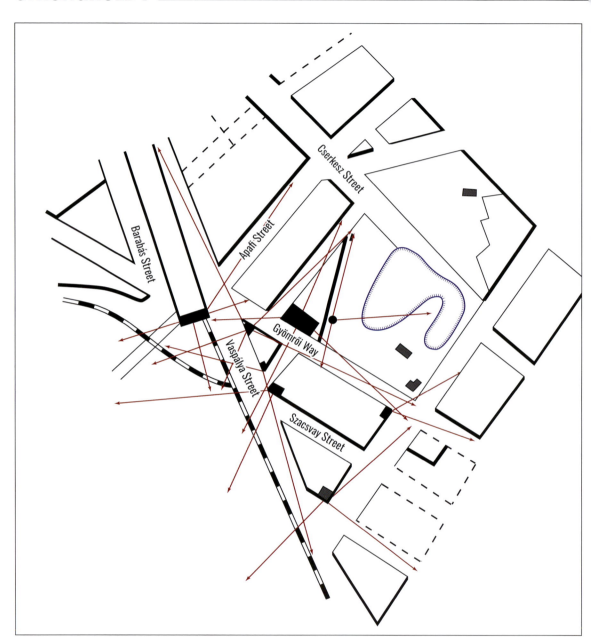

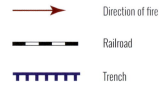

Fortress Budapest | Strongholds

The stronghold was situated on the southwestern limits of Kőbánya. It controlled an intersection of five streets, and in so doing protected the southern and western parts of the district. The stronghold was well suited for defence. (In front of it there was a clear, open space that was 0.5 km wide.) The nucleus of the stronghold were several solid buildings.

A strongpoint in an unfinished house.

A structure made of brick.

The wide, open space in front of the stronghold.

The wide, open space in front of the stronghold.

Brickworks.

STRONGHOLD 8

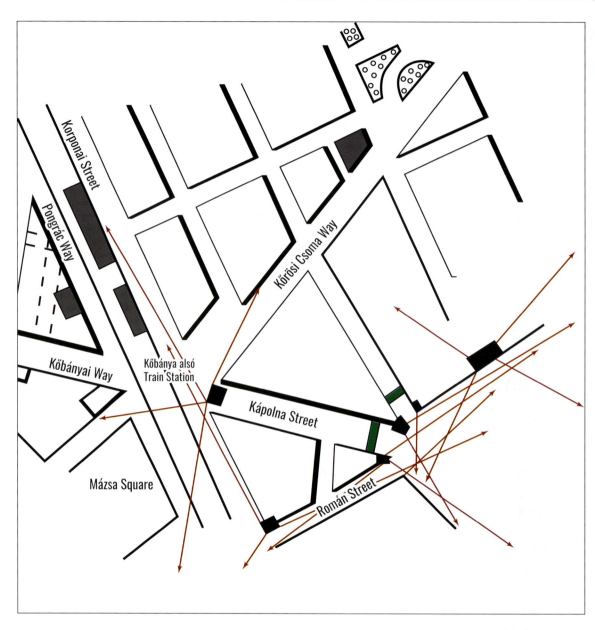

The stronghold was situated to the south of Kőbánya alsó train station.

The Reformed - Lutheran Church on Kápolna Street.

The Dreher Brewery protected Kápolna Street from the east.

Román Street was protected by the Reformed - Lutheran Church.

The corner building on the intersection of Kápolna and Román Streets was to interact with the strongpoint built in the Reformed - Lutheran Church.

STRONGHOLD 9

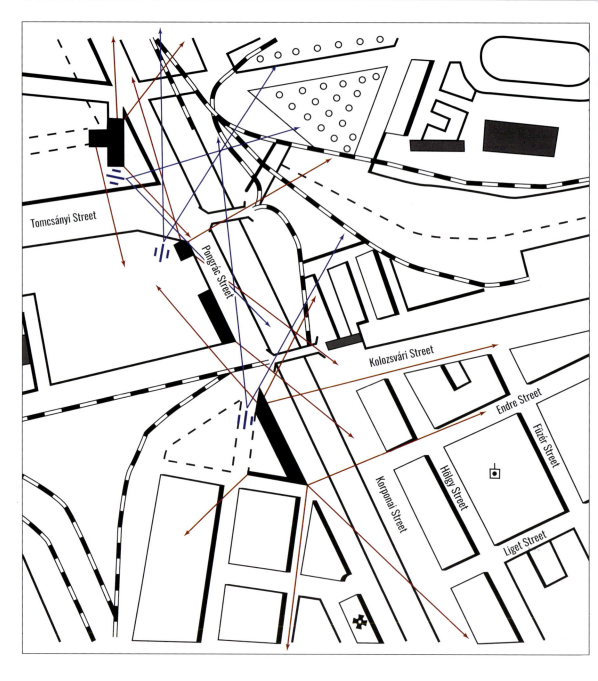

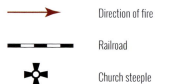

The stronghold was situated to the north of Kőbánya alsó Train Station. It consisted of several multi-storey residential stone buildings. There was a wide open space to the east of it (the New Racecourse). The stronghold controlled three main avenues leading to the city centre.

A firing point set up in one of the houses.

A residental building controlling the approaches to the railroad.

A residental building controlling the approaches to the railroad.

STRONGHOLD 10

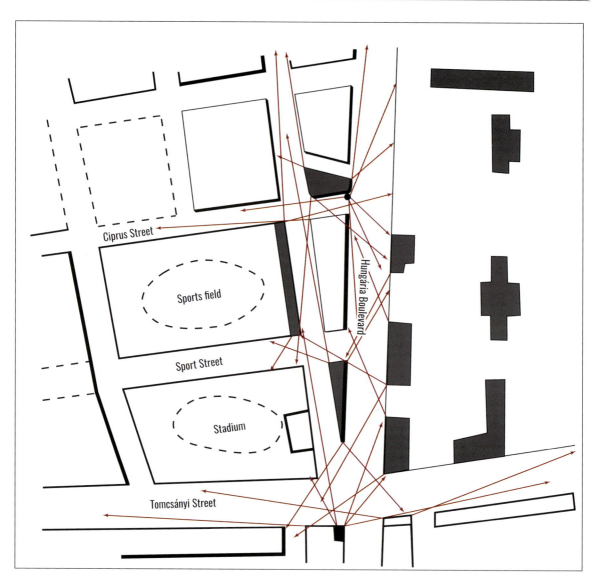

Direction of fire

The factory yard was protected by artillery and machine gun fire. (Mutually supporting firing points were set up in the factory building.) The defence of the yard was facilitated by the wide, open space to the southwest (BESZKÁRT and MOVE Sports Grounds) and by the existing iron-concrete structures.

A view of the factory yard.

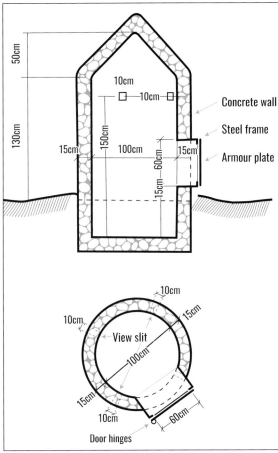

An artillery position in the factory's stokehold. It cooperated with the firing point in the iron-concrete structure (the air-raid shelter).

The yard was protected from the east by a factory building.

An iron-concrete structure in the factory yard that had been originally built as an air-raid shelter was used as a bunker.

STRONGHOLD 11

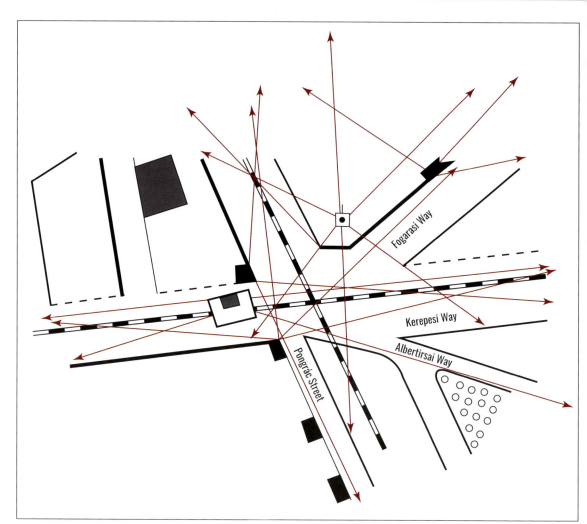

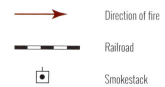

Fortress Budapest | Strongholds

Stronghold 11 protected an intersection of important avenues leading to the city centre, as well as the Budapest - Miskolc motorway. The multi-storey residential houses and the factory buildings, combined with the wide, open space in front of them facilitated the efforts of the defenders.

A view of the factory building.

A close view of the residential building on Fogarasi Way.	A close view of the residential building protecting Albertirsai Way and Pongrác Street.

STRONGHOLD 12

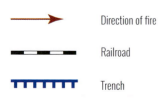

48

The stronghold was set up at the intersection of Hungária Boulevard and Egressy Way, and in so doing protected the approaches to the city centre. Since the number of the tall buildings in that area was insignifficant, the stronghold was additionaly reinforced with a trench line.

A view of the intersection.

A view of the intersection.

A view of the intersection.

STRONGHOLD 12

The building and the trenchline dug out along the western side of Hungária Boulevard.

A two-storey building protecting the northwestern corner of the intersection.

A four-storey building controlling a defensive sector that was 1-km long.

A rifle-squad position built in the attic of a garage made of brick.

An artillery position under the arches of the water tower.

Water tower.

Fortress Budapest | Strongholds

The segment of Hungária Boulevard to the north of Egressy Way was controlled by a strongpoint consisting of a five-storey building and several small houses/buildings.

A view of the field of fire (the wide, open space between the Main Post Office and the lower part of Stefánia Way) from the artillery position at the water tower.

STRONGHOLD 13

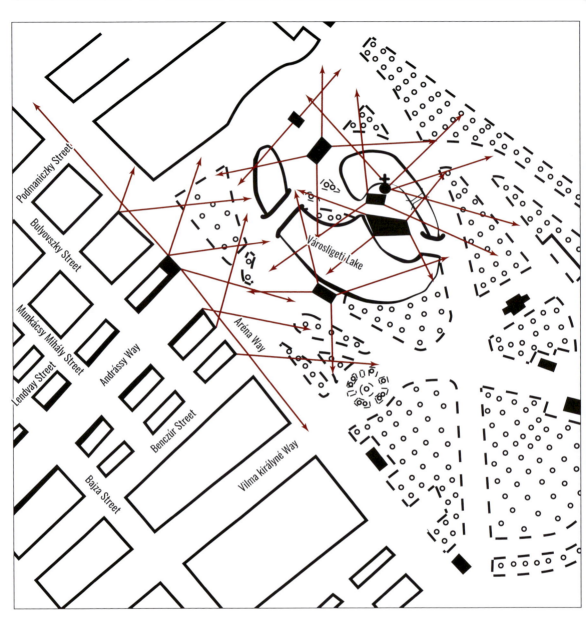

The Museum of Hungarian Agriculture (also known as Vajdahunyad Castle) was transformed into a stronghold protecting the approaches to the main avenues of the city, Andrássy Way and Aréna Way. The defence was facilitated by the lake surrounding the castle (it was about 50 m wide and 1.2 - 1.5 m deep). The gates, the entrances and the bridges were closed by a stone barricade that was 1.2 m high and 2 m thick.

The windows and the entrances of this building (on Aréna Way) were prepared for defence.

Tower with loopholes and remnants of a barricade.

Reinforced windows used as firing points.

The gates and the tower protecting them.

A building protected by a barricade.

Corner tower with fortified windows.

Corner tower with fortified windows.

STRONGHOLD 14

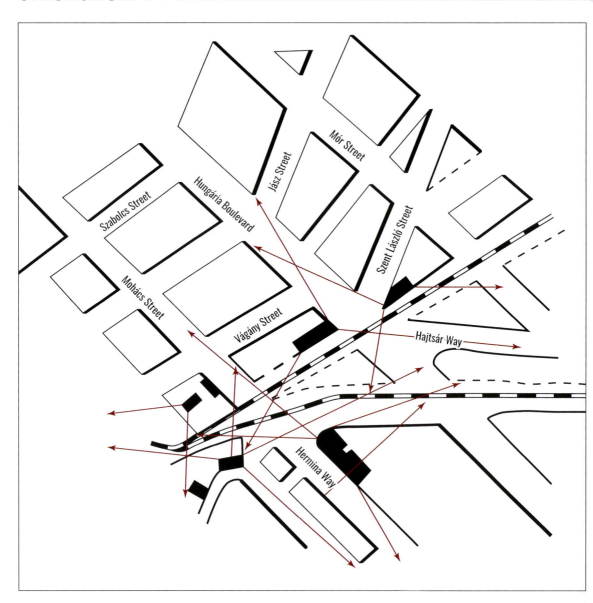

The intersection of Róbert Károly Boulevard and Hajtsár Street, and the railroad fork, were protected by the stone buildings at the corner, as well as by smaller service buildings.

A view of the stronghold.

The approaches to the railroad were also under the control of the stronghold.

A solid residental building protecting the intersection of Vágány Street, Róbert Károly Boulevard and Hajtsár Street.

STRONGHOLD 15

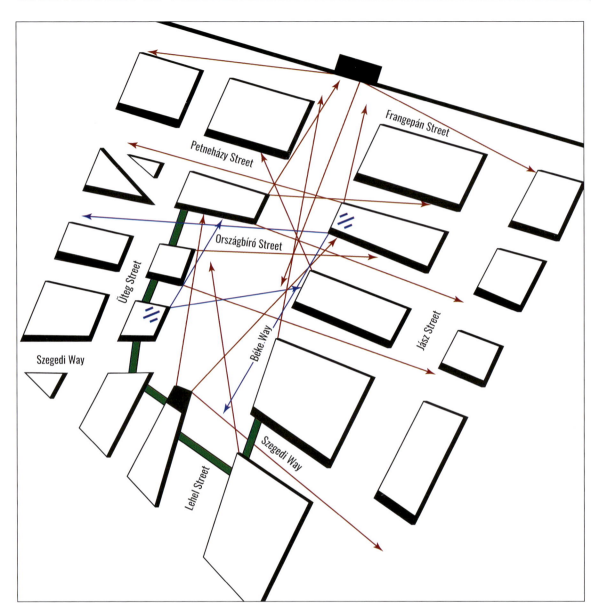

Direction of fire

Roadblock

Artillery gun

Béke Square controlled simultaneously six streets. The square was defended by barricades erected at the intersections and buildings turned into strongpoints.

A view of Béke Square.

A firing point (silenced by the Soviet artillery).

A firing point (silenced by the Soviet artillery).

A view of Szegedi Way.

A building protected by a barricade.

An artillery position behind a fence.

STRONGHOLD 16

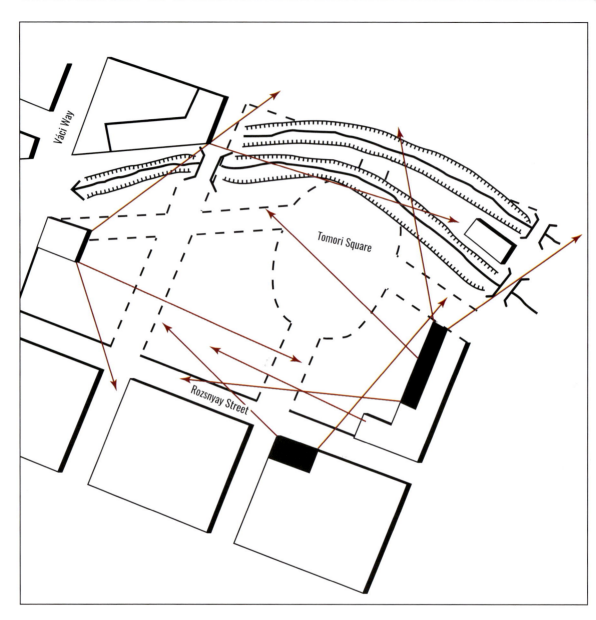

The large Tomori Square (1 km x 1.5 km) was protected by a group of three-storey residential houses. The Rákos Stream (which was 6-8 m wide and 2-2.5 m deep) was employed as an anti-tank ditch.

A view of Tomori Square.

The Rákos Stream.

The Rákos Stream.

A blown-up bridge that had been spanning the Rákos Stream.

STRONGHOLD 17

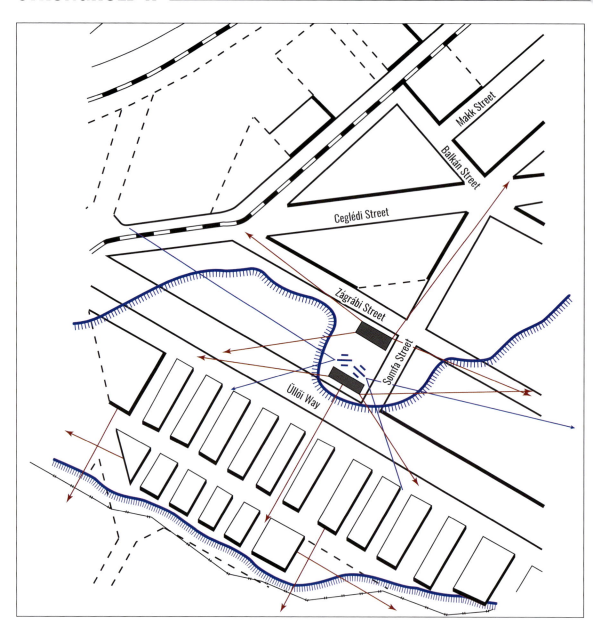

This stronghld was situated in the southwestern part of Kőbánya. Its main purpose was to control Geglédi Way. Its nucleus was made up of four 4-storey buildings. The buildings were interconnected by a trench line situated some 100-150 m from them. Apart from that, the stronghold was also prepared for all-around defence.

One of the main buildings of the stronghold, which had received 52 artillery hits. The middle part of the stronghold was girded by a trench line.

The middle part of the stronghold.

STRONGHOLD 18

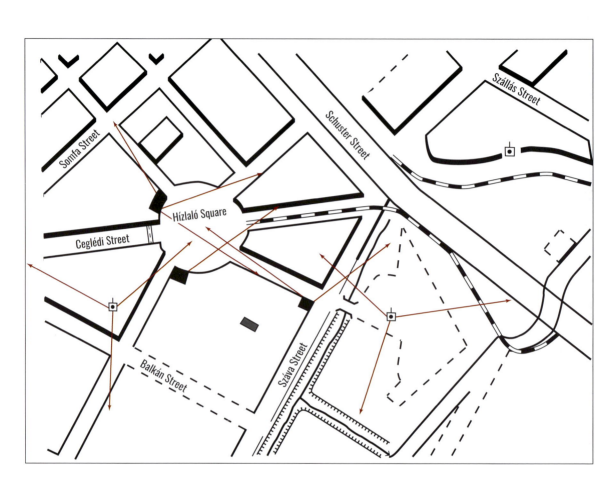

In the southwestern part of Kőbánya there was an open space that was 1-1.5 km long. It was protected by a system of fortified residential houses and factory buildings.

An artillery position built in the entrance of a warehouse/factory.

An artillery position built in the entrance of a warehouse/factory.

A stone house converted into a firing point. It was used as an emplacement for a heavy machine gun.

STRONGHOLD 19

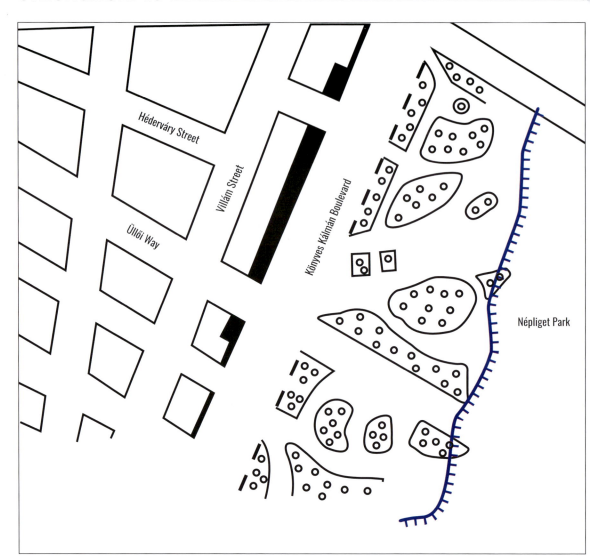

▬▬▬▬▬▬ Trench

The Ethnographic Museum, which had very thick walls, was easily transformed into a stronghold. Its defence was additionally facilitated by the wide, open space and Népliget Park in front of the building. It took the Soviets three days to fully secure the museum.

A side view of the museum.

A front view of the museum.

A view of the museum.

The wide, open space in front of the museum and the trenches occupied by the Soviet troops.

STRONGHOLD 20

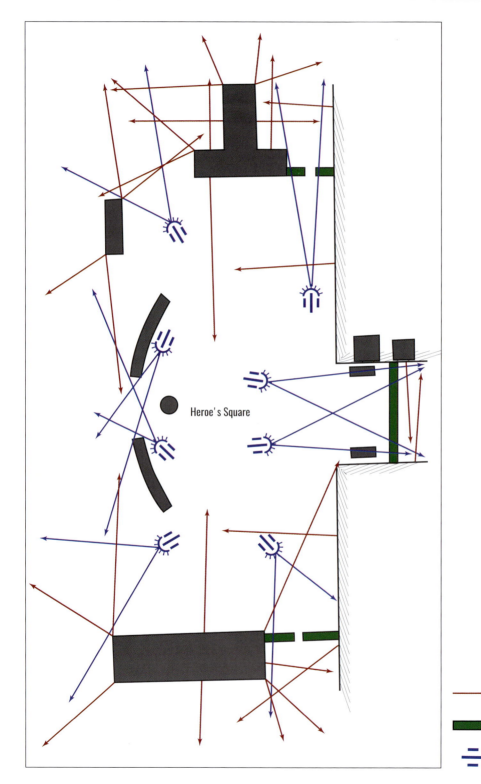

Fortress Budapest | Strongholds

Heroes' Square was transformed into a stronghold that blocked the access to Andrássy Way and protected the flanks of the bridgehead along Aréna Way. The Museum of Fine Arts and the Hall of Art, as well as several gun emplacements made of stone, were integrated into the defence system. The approaches to the square were screened by barricades. The barricades themselves were covered by fire from machine guns sited in the nearby buildings.

A view of the square.

STRONGHOLD 21

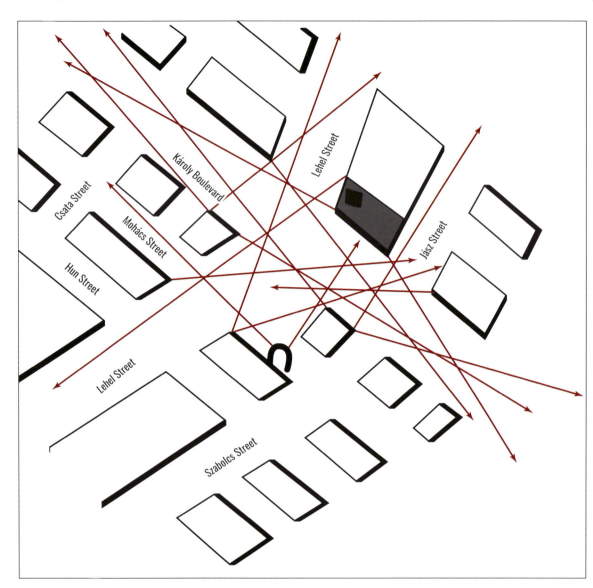

→ Direction of fire

Fortress Budapest | Strongholds

The stronghold protecting the intersection of Lehel Street and Róbert Károly Boulevard consisted of barricades and multistorey buildings. This allowed the defenders to keep under fire all likely approaches to it.

The mental asylum had been turned into a strongpoint defending the intersection.

A makeshift artillery position.

An iron-concrete structure that had been originally built as a stand-alone air-raid shelter was integrated into the stronghold as a bunker.

STRONGHOLD 22

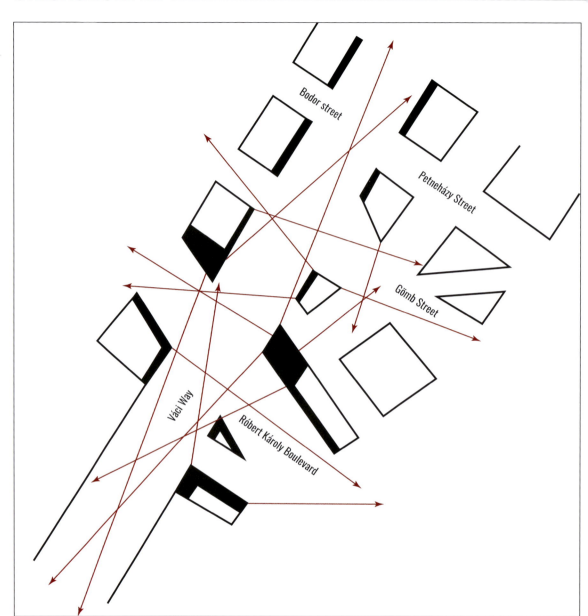

The stronghold set up at the intersection of Váci Way and Róbert Károly Boulevard barred access to the city centre from the north, along the Vác - Budapest motorway.

A view of the intersection.

There was a wide, open space between the intersection and the Danube bank.

The core of the stronghold was the warehouse in the northeastern corner of the intersection.

STRONGHOLD 23

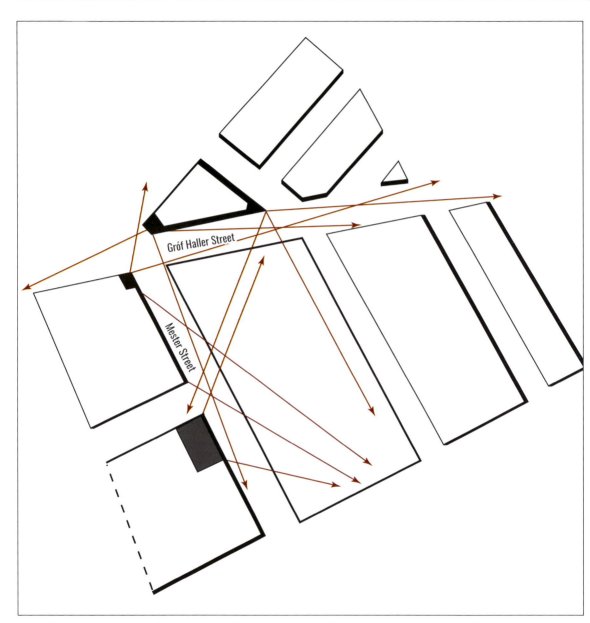

Direction of fire

Stronghold 23 controlled the vicinity of the intersection of Haller and Mester Streets, and barred access to two of the main bridges (Horthy Miklós Bridge and Ferenc József Bridge). It consisted of solid residental corner buildings, a church and attics turned into firing points.

This group of buildings and the church protected Mester Street and the intersection.

These corner buildings protected simultaneously two streets and the intersection.

STRONGHOLD 24

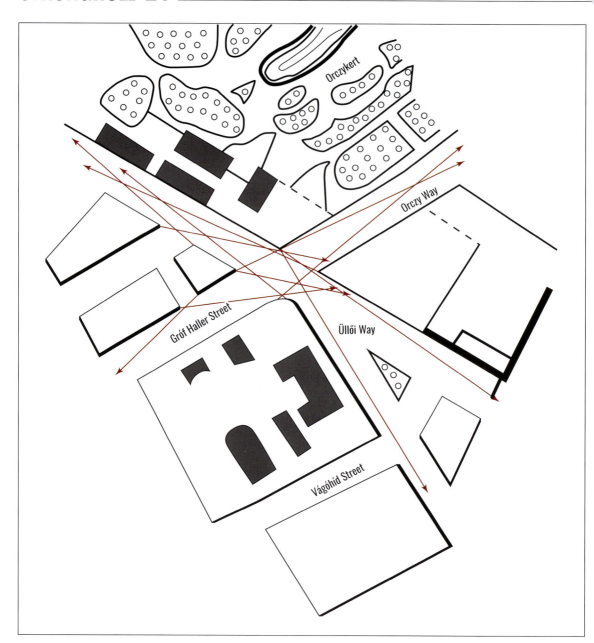

Direction of fire

74

Fortress Budapest | Strongholds

Nagyvárad Square (the intersection of Üllői Way, Haller Steet and Orczy Way) was protected by the stone residential buildings surrounding it. Barricades were employed as anti-tank obstacles.

A large residential building used to protect the square.

A view of Üllői Way and the square.

A view of the square.

STRONGHOLD 25

Guns on armoured flatcars.

An artillery position made of cable reels and cement bags.

An artillery position made of barrels of paint and gypsum bags.

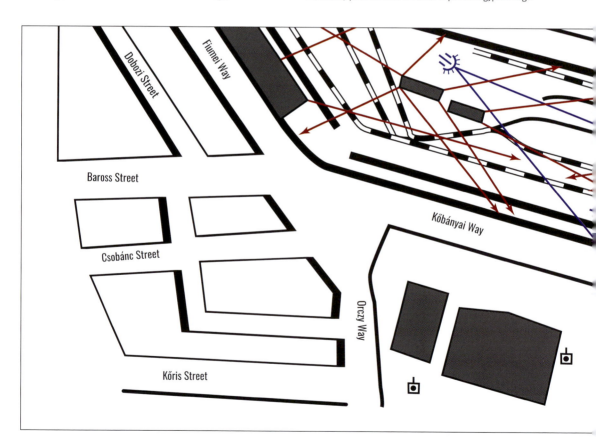

→ Direction of fire   ▬ Railroad   ▮ Armoured railway cars as artillery platforms   ▣ Smokestack

Fortress Budapest | Strongholds

Józsefvárosi Railway Terminal was transformed into a solid artillery stronghold. The guns were installed on armoured flatcars or in makeshift horseshoe-shaped emplacements. (The latter were made of cable reels, cement bags and gypsum bags.) Iron-concrete fence and boxcars filled with metal scrap were used as anti-personnel and anti-tank obstacles.

Boxcars filled with metal scrap used as obstacles.

An artillery position made of gypsum bags.

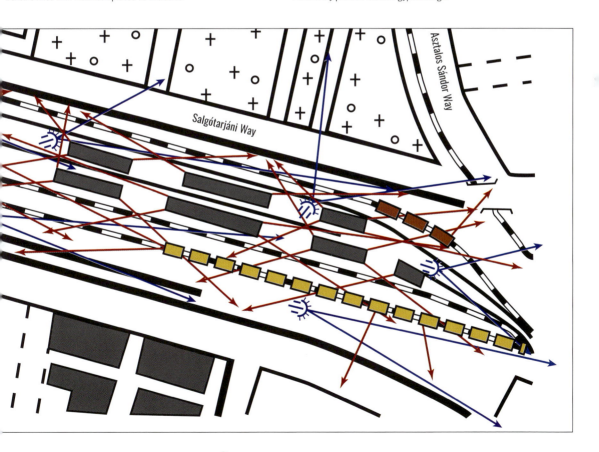

■ Railway cars filled with metallic material   ⋺ Artillery gun

STRONGHOLD 26

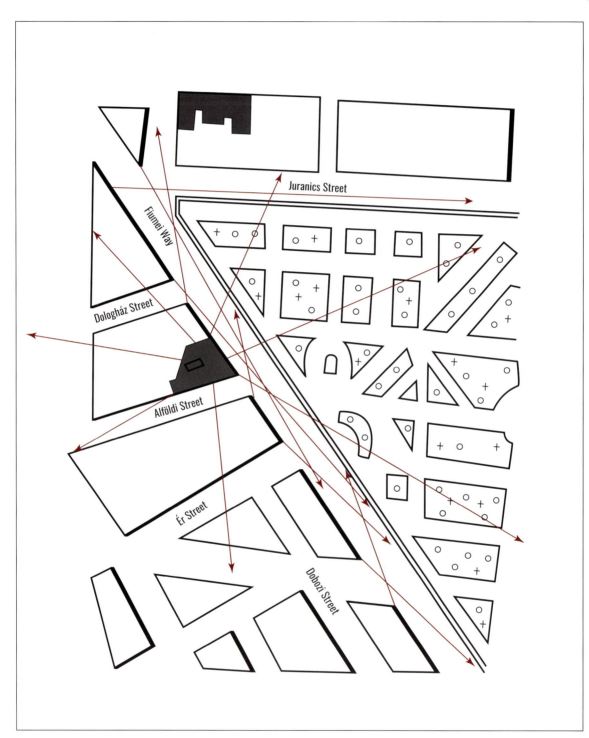

→ Direction of fire

The twelve-storey building of the National Social Insurance Institute commanded the neighborhood of Kerepesi Cemetery. Because of that it was employed as both an observation post and firing point. The defence of the cemetery was facilitated by an iron-concrete fence. The cemetery itself was transformed into a stronghold. The railroad on Asztalos Sándor Street (along its eastern side) was defended by medium artillery pieces firing through gunports cut in the cemetery wall.

The National Social Insurance Institute.

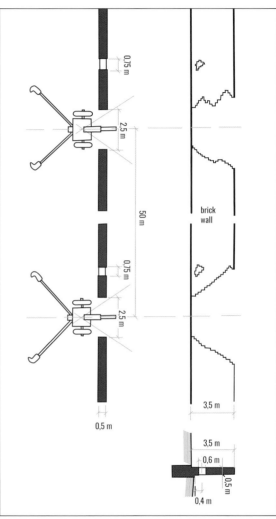

The National Social Insurance Institute.

A gunport cut in the cemetery wall.

STRONGHOLD 27

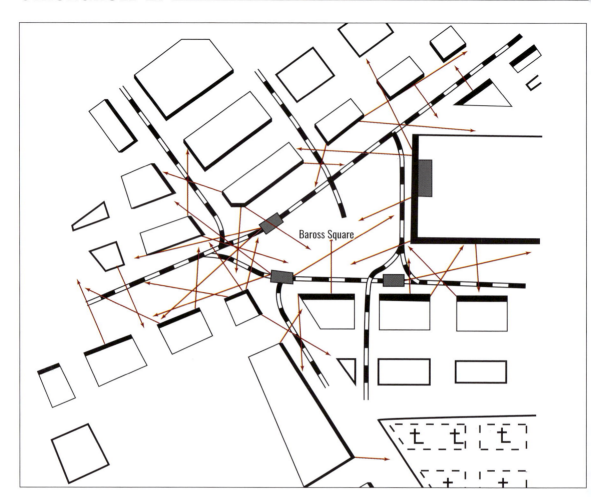

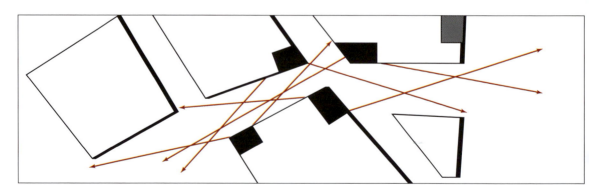

Direction of fire

Railroad

Fortress Budapest | Strongholds

Baross Square and Keleti Terminal barred the access to Rákóczi Way, Rottenbiller Street and Fiumei Way. The stronghold was defended predominately by means of armoured railcars. Three types of armoured railcars were placed on the square: 1) outfitted with machine guns; 2) outfitted with auto-cannons; 3) outfitted with medium-caliber guns. The employment of the armoured railcars in the city centre was made possible because the tram used the same gauge as the rail system.

Baross Square was also protected by multi-storey residential buildings whose attics had been transformed into air-raid shelters. They also barred access to the streets leading to the downtown part of the city.

A view on the square.   Buildings of Baross Square 1 and Rákóczi Way 75.

An armoured railcar outfitted with a medium-caliber gun.   An armoured railcar outfitted with machine guns.

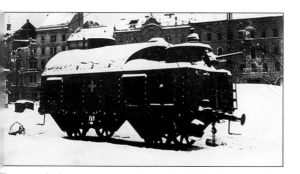

An armoured railcar outfitted with an auto-cannon.

STRONGHOLD 28

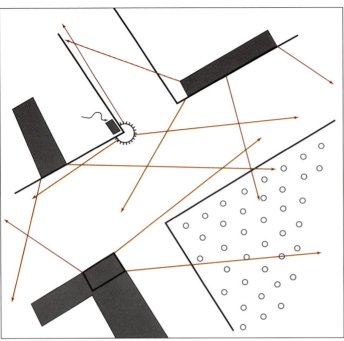
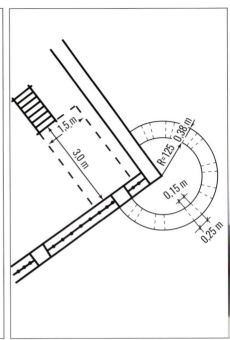
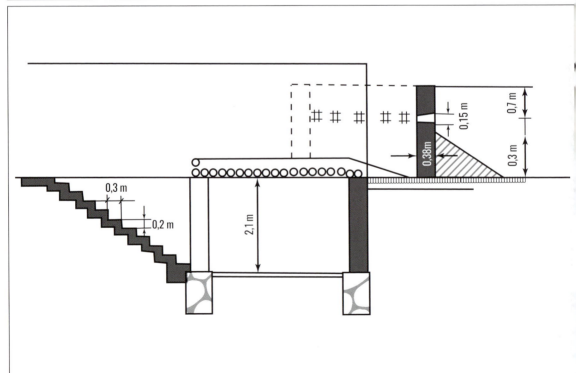

Direction of fire

The stronghold was made of two solid buildings: Railway Barracks and Archduke Albrecht Barracks.

Location as shown on the accompanying map.

Location as shown on the accompanying map.

STRONGHOLD 29

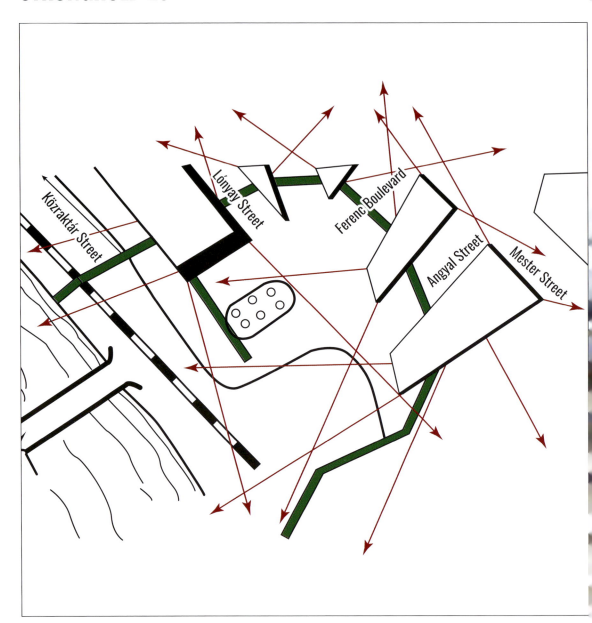

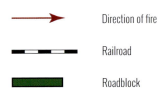

84

Boráros Square was transformed into a stronghold barring the access to Horthy Miklós Bridge. Several solid residential buildings and a number of "dragon teeth" obstacles constituted the core of the defence.

"Dragon's teeth" at Horthy Miklós Bridge.

"Dragon's teeth" at Horthy Miklós Bridge.

These residential buildings protected the approaches to the bridge.

STRONGHOLD 30

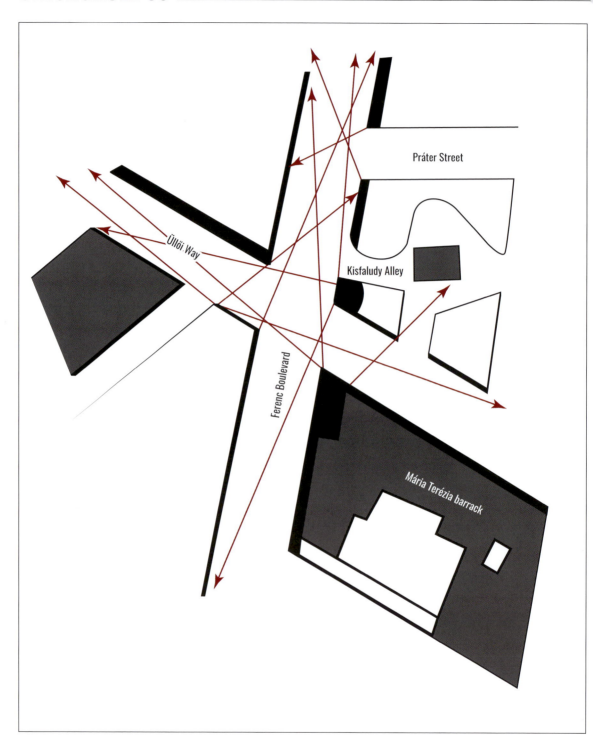

→ Direction of fire

The stronghold built at the intersection of Grand Boulevard (Ferenc Boulevard/József Boulevard) and Üllői Way barred the access to Horthy Miklós Bridge. It was made of several solid corner buildings, including Maria Theresa Barracks.

ZiS-3 76.2-mm gun of 66th Guards Rifle Division on Üllői Way. To the left is the building of the Museum of Applied Arts.

Soviet troops passing by an abandoned PAK 40 anti-tank gun on József Avenue. The Kisfaludy Square can be seen in the background (today: Corvin Square).

STRONGHOLD 30

Fallen German soldier on Üllői Way, in front of the Museum of Applied Arts.

Fallen German soldier on Üllői Way, in front of the Museum of Applied Arts.

Soviet troops on József Boulevard.

STRONGHOLD 31

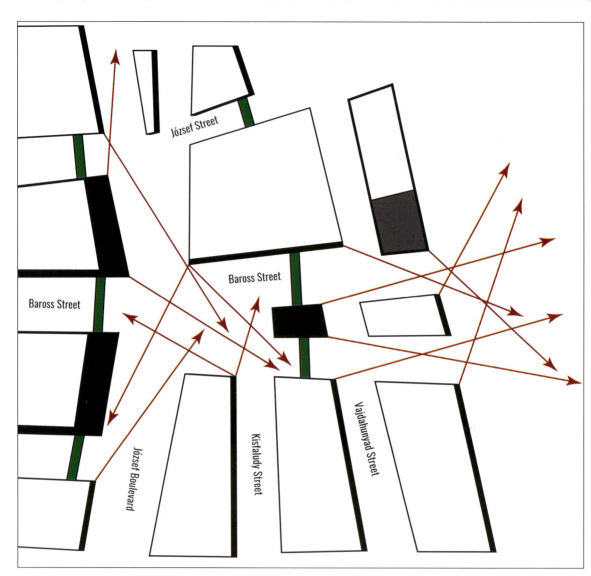

→ Direction of fire

▬ Roadblock

The stronghold built at Harminckettesek Square (the intersection of József Boulevard and Baross Street) barred the access to Horthy Miklós Bridge and Ferenc József Bridge. It consisted of barricades made of various materials and solid residental buildings.

The building on the corner of József Boulevard and Baross Street.

STRONGHOLD 32

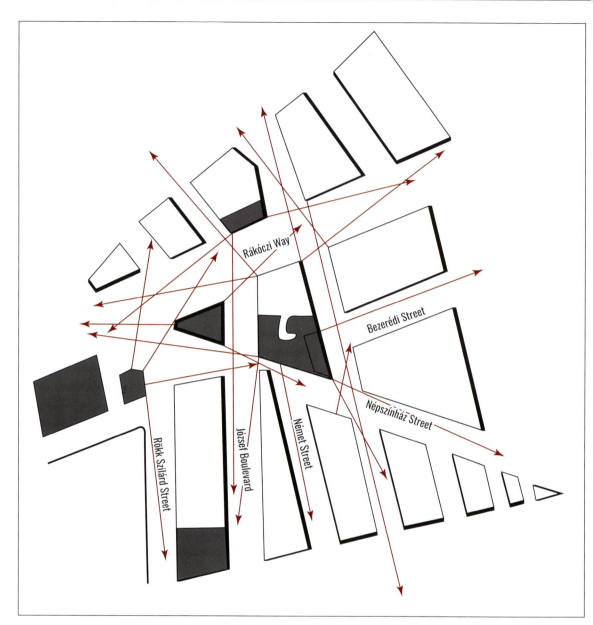

→ Direction of fire

Fortress Budapest | Strongholds

The stronghold at Blaha Lujza Square protected simultaneosly two main boulevards: Rákóczi Way and the Grand Boulevard. Thanks to the considerable number of solid buildings surrounding the square, as well as the barricades erected on the streets, and especially by the disposition of the buildings in the square, the stronghold could be defended by a relatively small force.

One of the buildings and the roadblock which defended the crossroads.

The building at the crossroads of Rákóczi Way and Erzsébet Boulevard.

Budapest, Rákóczi Way 42 - today EMKE Business Centre.

The Akácfa Street at Blaha Lujza Square.

STRONGHOLD 33 AND 34

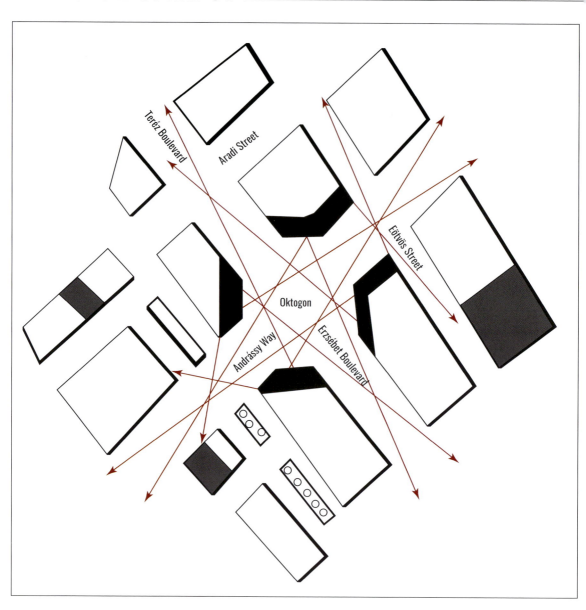

Direction of fire

The stronghold at Mussolini Square protected downtown Pest by simultaneosly barring two main avenues: Andrássy Way and the Grand Boulevard. The defence of these thoroughfares was facilitated by the solid buildings surrounding the square and the erected barricade.

Fortress Budapest | Strongholds

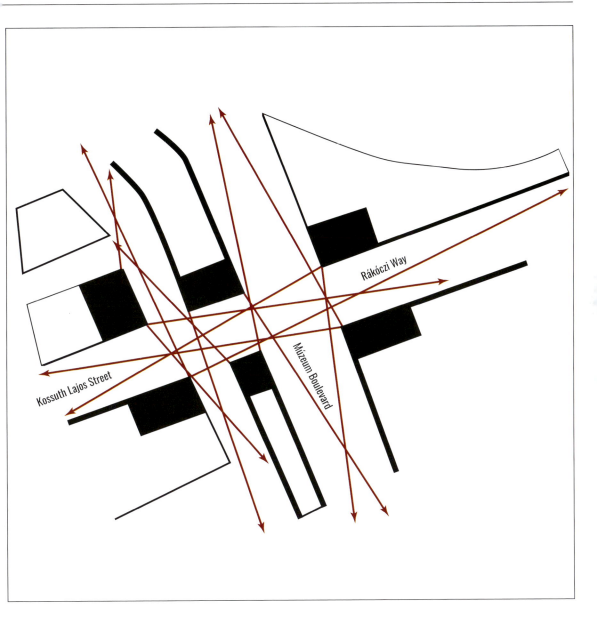

→ Direction of fire

The stronghold set up at the intersection of the Small Boulevard and Rákóczi Way barred the approaches to Erzsébet Bridge.

STRONGHOLD 35

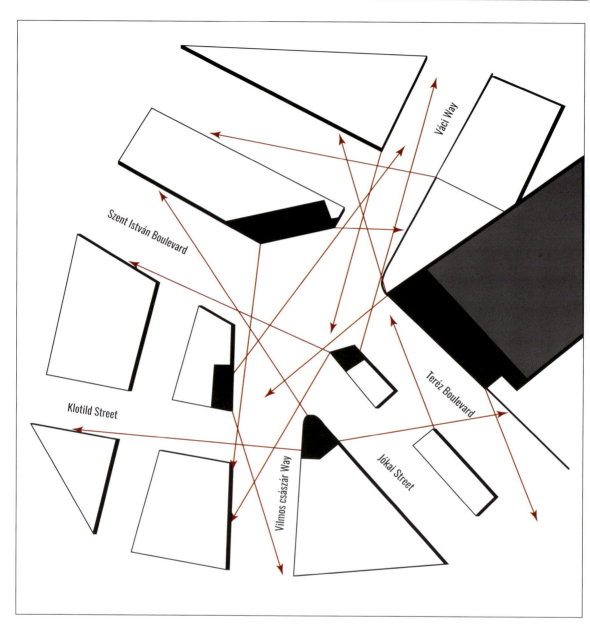

Direction of fire

The distant approaches to Margit Bridge were protected by a stronghold set up at Berlin Square. It simultaneously controlled four main avenues: Szent István Boulevard, Váci Way, Vilmos császár Way and Teréz Boulevard. Adjacent to the square was Nyugati Railway Terminal, which was fortified with a barricade. The entrances to the terminal were blocked by brick walls that were 1.5 m thick and 1.2-1.5 m high.

A barricade at the terminal.

A barricade at the terminal.

Buildings used to defend the square.

Buildings used to defend the square.

STRONGHOLD 36

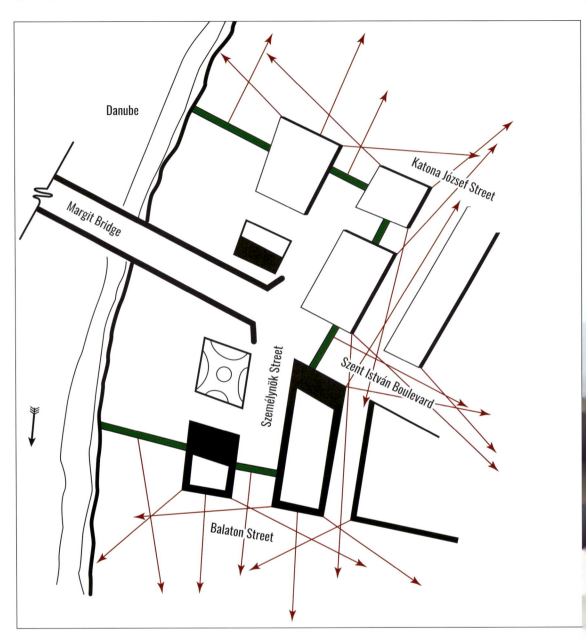

Fortress Budapest | Strongholds

The eastern bridgehead of Margit Bridge was protected by a stronghold made of solid residential buildings and barricades.

Barricaded pedestrian underpass under the bridgehead.

Barricade on the Balassi Bálint Street, which closed the bridgehead from the parliament.

Barricade on the road running under the bridgehead.

Falk Miksa Street.

STRONGHOLD 37

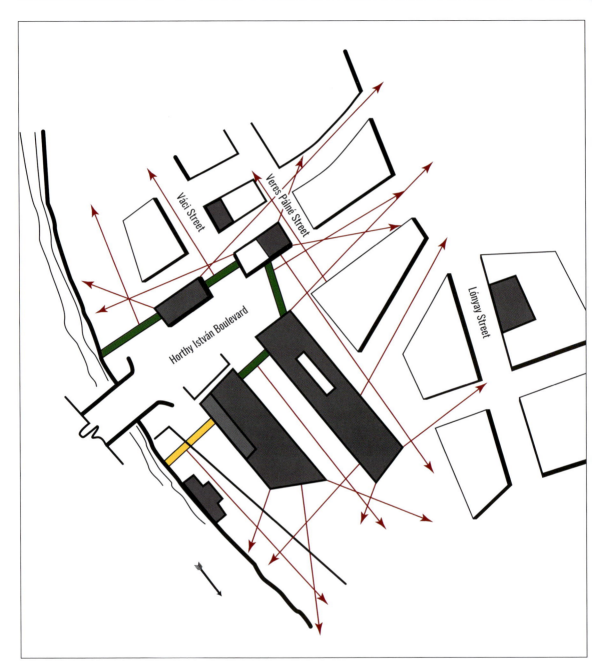

Direction of fire

Roadblock

Barriers and obstacles

The eastern bridgehead of Ferenc József Bridge was protected by a stronghold made of solid residential buildings, "dragon's teeth", iron anti-tank obstacles, barricades and barbed-wire entanglements.

"Dragon's teeth" at the end of Váci Street

Molnár Street at Fővám Square with the statue of 1. honvéd és népfölkelő gyalogezred (1. Home Defence and Militia Infantry Regiment).

The Great Market Place (Nagy Vásárcsarnok) seen from Sóház Street

STRONGHOLD 38

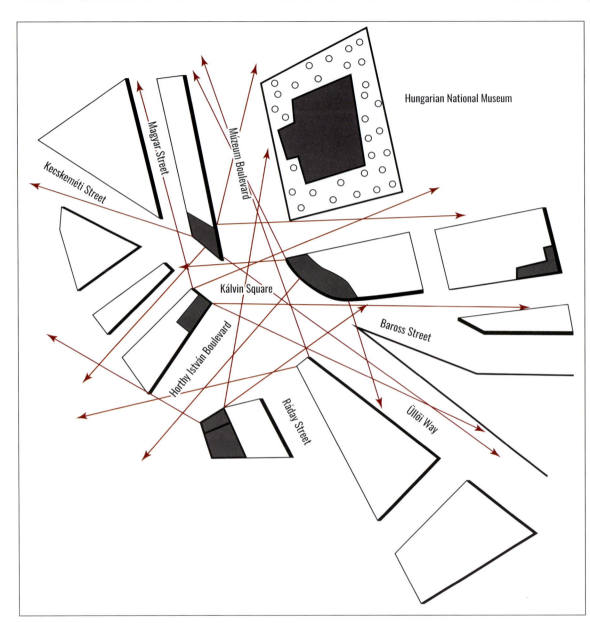

The approaches to Ferenc József Bridge along the main streets were protected by a stronghold set up at Kálvin Square. The solid stone buildings surronding the square allowed the defenders to hold the perimeter without carrying out any additional fortification works.

A building (Pintér-ház) protecting the square.

A building (Pintér-ház) protecting the square.

A building protecting the square.

The Üllői Way at Kálvin Square.

STRONGHOLD 38

The Metropolitan Library Szabó Ervin.

Fortress Budapest | Strongholds

Horthy István Boulevard (today: Vámház Boulevard).

Hungarian National Museum

STRONGHOLD 39

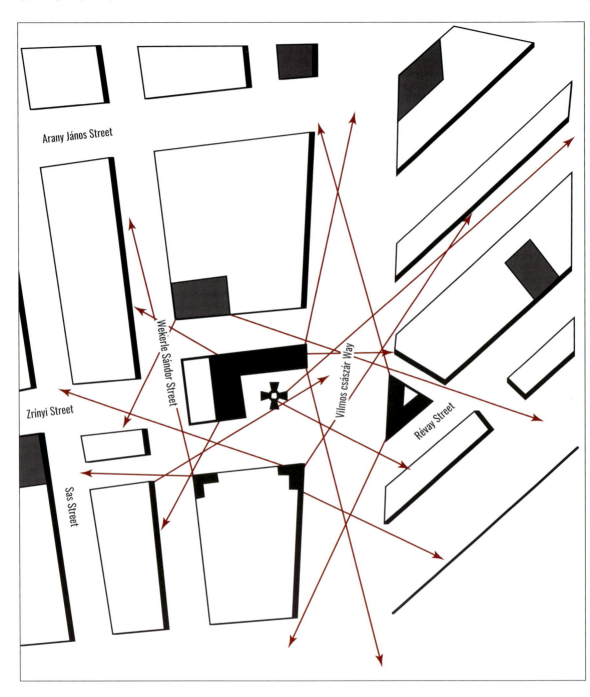

  Direction of fire

Church steeple

The stronghold set up at Szent István Square protected the approaches to Széchenyi Chain Bridge. The main buildings within the stronghold were employed for defence. In particular, St. Stephen's Basilica and the multistorey residential house on the corner of Vilmos császár Way and Révay Street provided each other with mutual support.

Zrínyi Street and St. Stephen's Basilica.

STRONGHOLD 40

Direction of fire

The stronghold set up at Szabadság Square protected the approaches to Széchenyi Chain Bridge from the north and northeast. Barricades were erected on the square and the ground floors of the buildings were fortified.

A view of the square.

A barricade made of car wrecks in Nádor Street.

STRONGHOLD 40

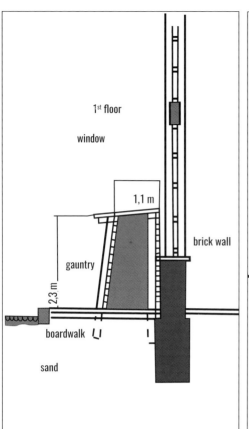
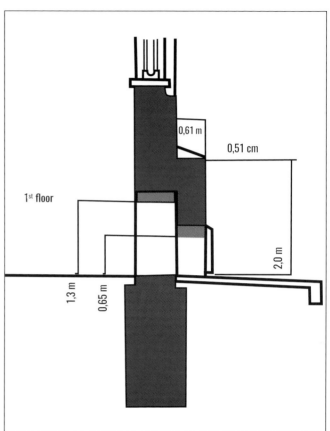
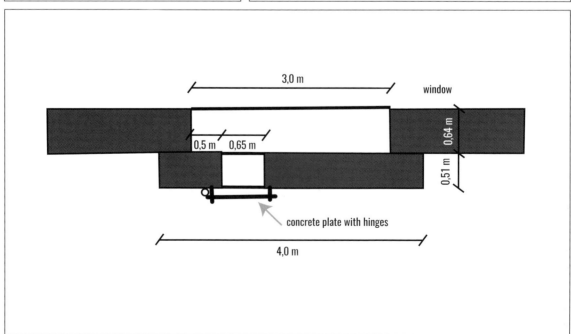

Strengthened ground floor of an office building.

Strengthened ground floor of an office building.

Strengthened ground floor of an office building.

STRONGHOLD 41

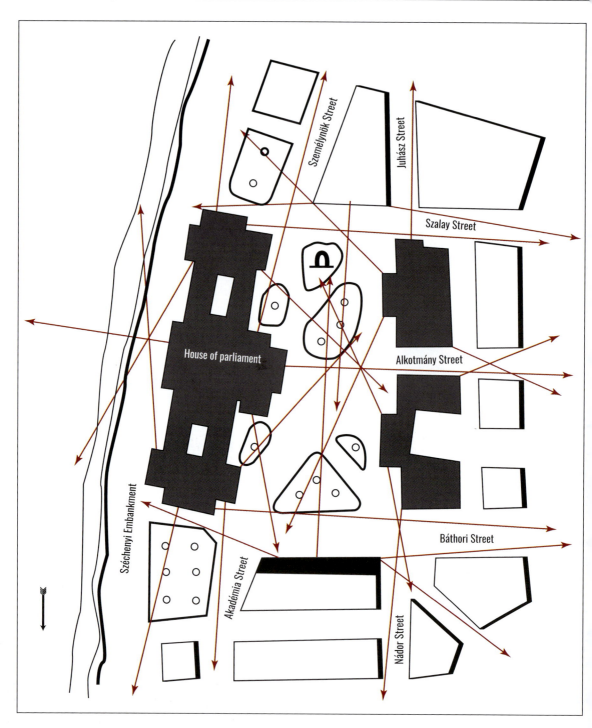

Direction of fire

The parliament and the stone buildings surrounding the parliament square were transformed into a formidable stronghold. It barred access to the embankment, and offered flank protection to Margit bridge and Széchenyi Chain Bridge. The narrow streets and the barricades erected on them made the stronghold a hard nut to crack.

The House of Parliament

STRONGHOLD 41

The Hungarian Royal Mansion (today: Ethnographic Museum).

The rear side of the Hungarian Royal Mansion (today: Ethnographic Museum).

STRONGHOLD 42

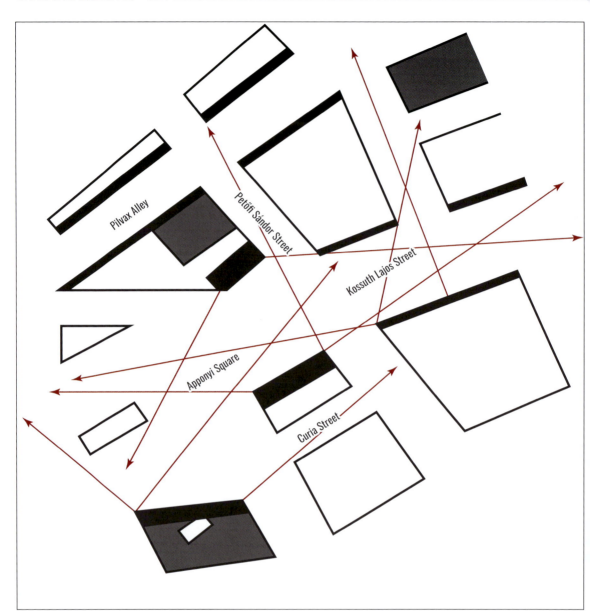

→ Direction of fire

Stronghold 42 at Apponyi Square protected the near approaches to Erzsébet Bridge. The narrow streets leading to the square and the tall, solid buildings further facilitated the defence.

The Werbőczy Statue in front of Párisi Udvar

The Párisi Udvar and the Northern Klotild Palace

Petőfi Sándor Street seen from Párisi Street

STRONGHOLD 43

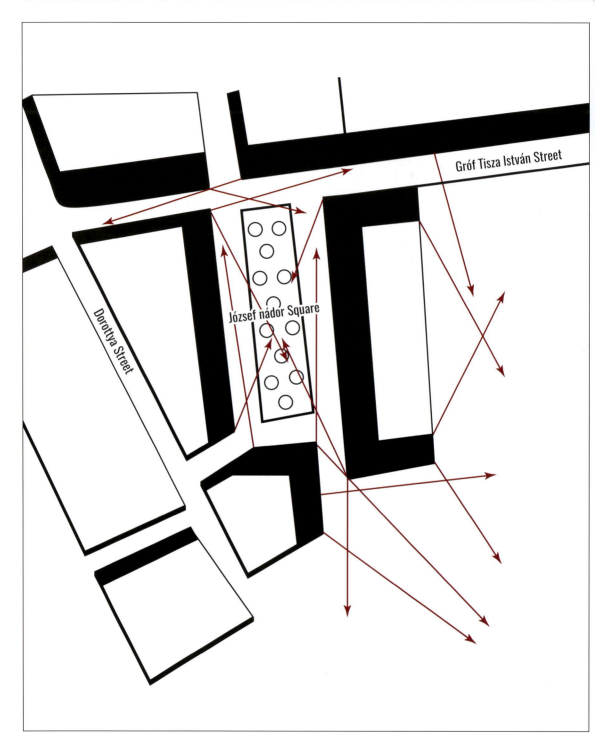

Direction of fire

The stronghold at József Square protected the near approaches to Széchenyi Chain Bridge. The windows of the ground floors were reinforced with sandbags. "Dragon's teeth" anti-tank obstacles were arranged in chess-like pattern.

Gróf Tisza István Street 8 (today: József Attila Street) at the Northern edge of József Nádor Square.

Statue of József Nádor in front of József Nádor Square 12.

Corner of József Nádor Square and Wekerle Sándor Street.

STRONGHOLD 44

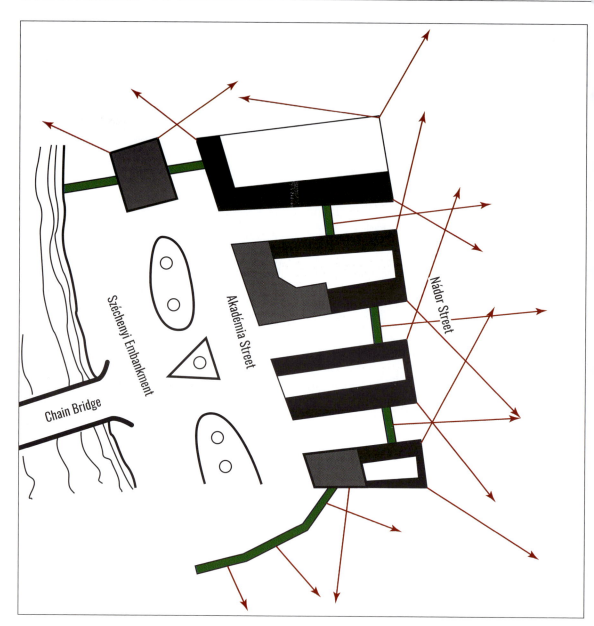

The stronghold at Ferenc József Square protected the near approaches to the Chain Bridge.

The Hungarian Academy of Sciences

The Hungarian Academy of Sciences and barricades set on the square.

STRONGHOLD 44

Lloyd Palace on Ferenc József Square (today: Széchenyi Square) at Dorottya Street.

Ferenc József Square (today: Széchenyi Square) seen from Zrínyi Street.

Fortress Budapest | Strongholds

Zrínyi Street and Ferenc József Square (today: Széchenyi Square)

"Dragon's teeth" on Gróf Tisza István Street (today: József Attila Street)

STRONGHOLD 45

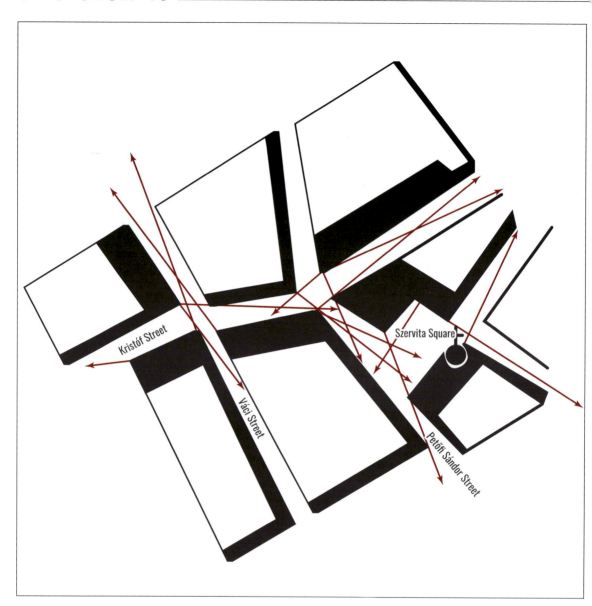

→ Direction of fire

☦ Chapel

The stronghold at Kristóf and Szervita Squares protected the near approaches to Erzsébet Bridge. They were surrounded by tall stone buildings transformed into mutually supporting strongpoints that could be held by relatively small forces.

Soviet troops in Bárczy István Street

Buildings in Városház Street

STRONGHOLD 46

A view on the freight section.

A view on the freight section.

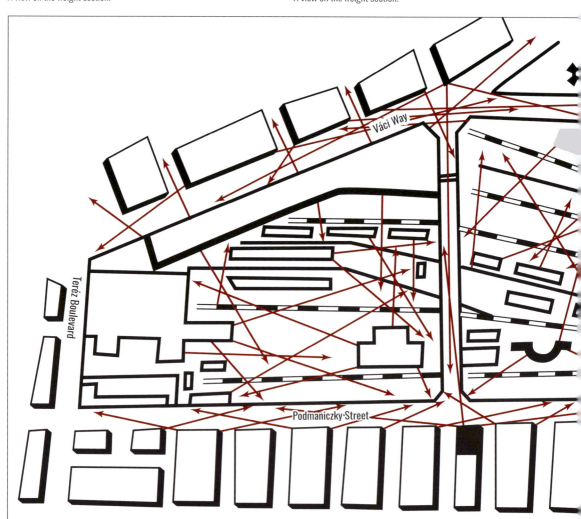

Fortress Budapest | Strongholds

The freight section of Nyugati railway terminal was situated to the east of the terminal's main building. It consisted of a marshalling yard and service buildings surrounded by a iron-concrete fence. The freight section was transformed into a stronghold that was nearly 2 km long and about 0.5 km wide.
The narrow streets and the tall, solid buildings in the neighborhood surrounding the terminal further facilitated the defence.

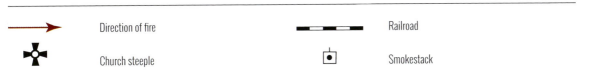

STRONGHOLD 47

The stronghold at Eskü and Petőfi Squares protected the near approaches to Erzsébet Bridge. It was reinforced with anti-tank obstacles and barbed-wire entanglements. The narrow streets and the tall, solid buildings girding the bridgehead further facilitated the defence.

The Church of Our Lady of downtown Budapest.

Eskü Square (today: Március 15. Square) with the remaining tower of the Hungarian Orthodox Cathedral in the background.

STRONGHOLD 47

Buildings on Eskü Square (today: Március 15. Square).

The Eastern bridgehead of Erzsébet Bridge.

"Dragon's teeth" placed in front of the bridge.

STRONGHOLD 48

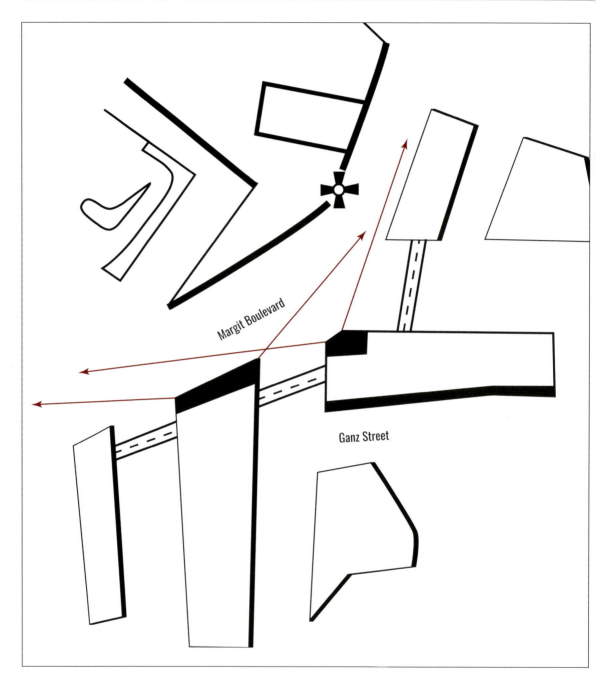

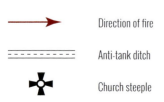

132

The stronghold at Mechwart Park barred the approaches to the Castle District. The multi-storey residential buildings on the southern side of Margit Boulevard proved to be very solid and withstood many artillery hits.

The four-story building of Margit Square 10 secured the approaches of the embankment of the Danube and defended part of Margit Boulevard.

The anti-tank ditch on Margit Boulevard was kept under fire from these buildings.

This six-story building at Margit Boulevard 46 was suitable for defence although it had been hit several times by artillery.

STRONGHOLD 49

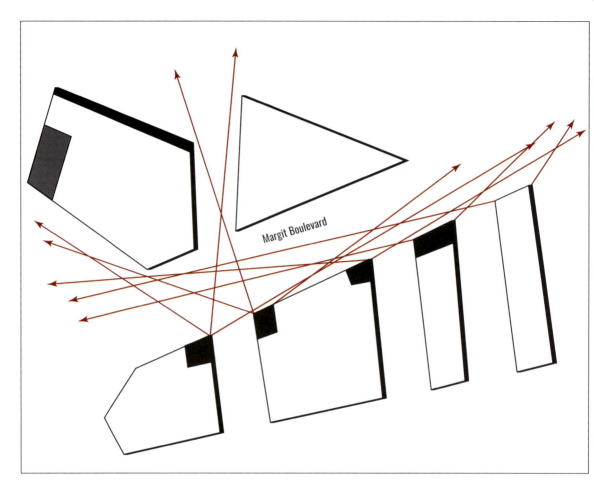

Direction of fire

Margit Boulevard was curvilinear, which allowed the defenders to keep the perimeter under fire from every building. The multi-storey buildings, with their thick walls and well-developed attics, offered good protection for the troops occupying them.

This multi-storey building (Margit Boulevard) barred the approaches to the castle district. The corner of the building shown on the photo had received more than 120 artillery hits.

A view onto Margit Boulevard. The specific way the buildings had been built allowed the defenders to keep it under intense flanking fire.

STRONGHOLD 50

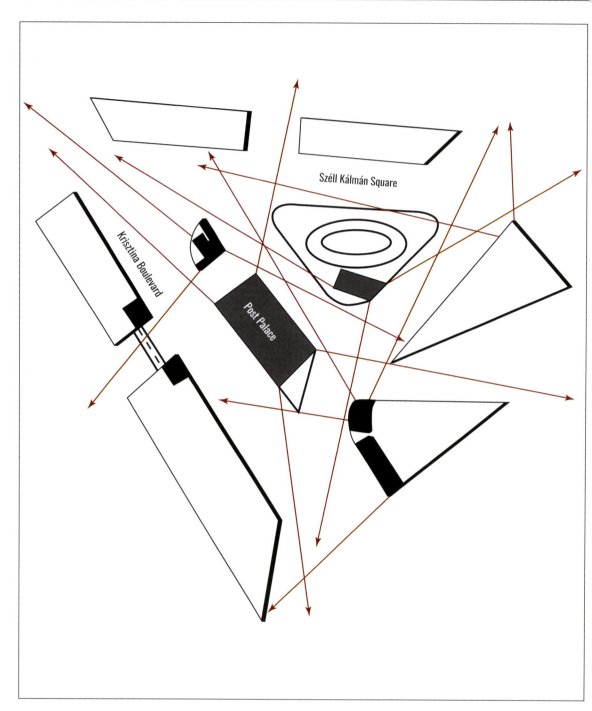

Fortress Budapest | Strongholds

This stronghold at Széll Kálmán Square barred the approaches to the Castle District from the northwest. It controlled simultneously three main avenues, thereby blocking the access to the downtown area of the city in that sector.

These five and six-story buildings were held by the defenders for 13 days although both the Soviet air force and artillery caused serious damage to them.

The German-Hungarian troops held this building at the corner of Vérmező Street and Várfok Street for 13 days.

A view of Széll Kálmán Square.

Both Krisztina Boulevard and Széll Kálmán Square could be controlled from the Post Palace.

Anti-tank ditch in Várfok Street kept under fire from the attic.

A damaged building at Széll Kálmán Square.

STRONGHOLD 51

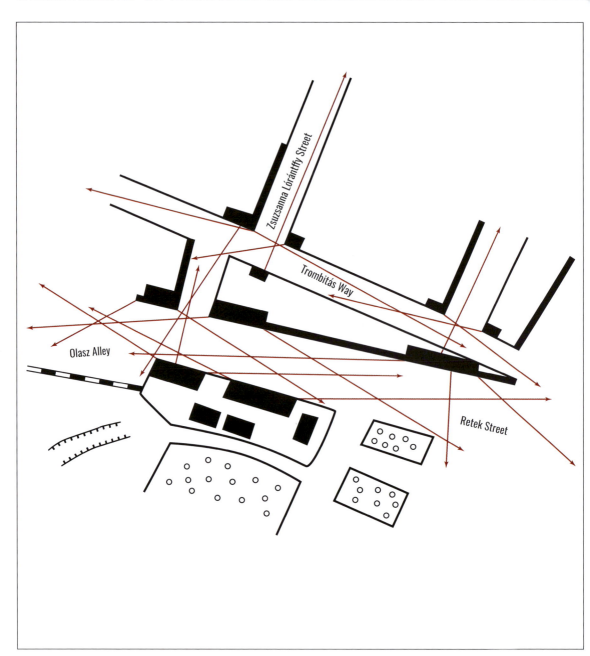

   Direction of fire

Railroad

The stronghold at the lower terminus of the cogwheel railway was made up of both multi-storey and single-storey buildings and houses with some empty spaces between them. By protecting Olasz Alley it barred the access to downtown Buda. It was reinforced with an anti-tank ditch, minefields and barbed-wire entanglements.

A stone building surrounded by a fence. Loopholes were cut in the fence to provide the artillery pieces with fields of fire.

A view of the building protecting Olasz Alley.

STRONGHOLD 52

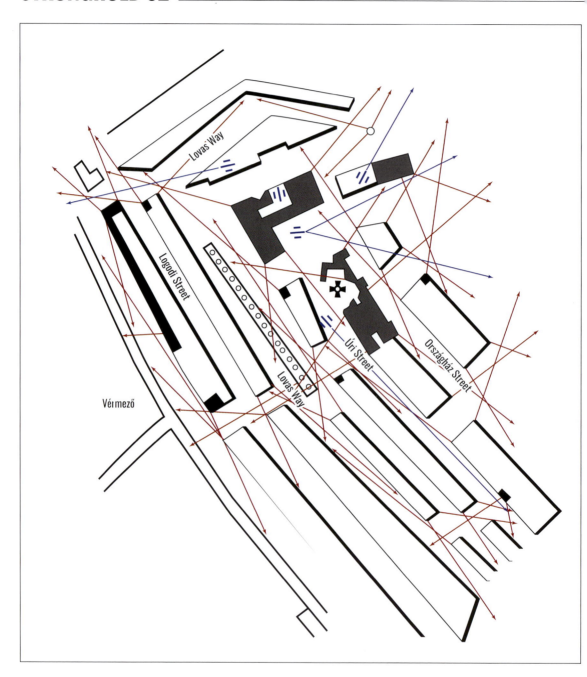

Direction of fire

Church steeple

Artillery gun

Fortress Budapest | Strongholds

The purpose of the stronghold at the Military Museum was to defend the Royal Pallace. It was made up of a number of stone buildings. The buildings of the Ministry of Interior, the State Archive and the other government buildings, which had been built on a commanding height, formed the core of the stronghold and controlled most of Buda. In front of the stronghold was Vérmező Meadow which was kept under constant fire from the buildings. The favorable terrain conditions and the thick stone walls made this stronhold a hard nut to crack.

The Hungarian National Archives.

STRONGHOLD 52

Kapisztrán Square

Mary Magdalene Church at Kapisztrán Square.

Bécsi Kapu Square (Vienna Gate Square).

The Military History Museum.

STRONGHOLD 53

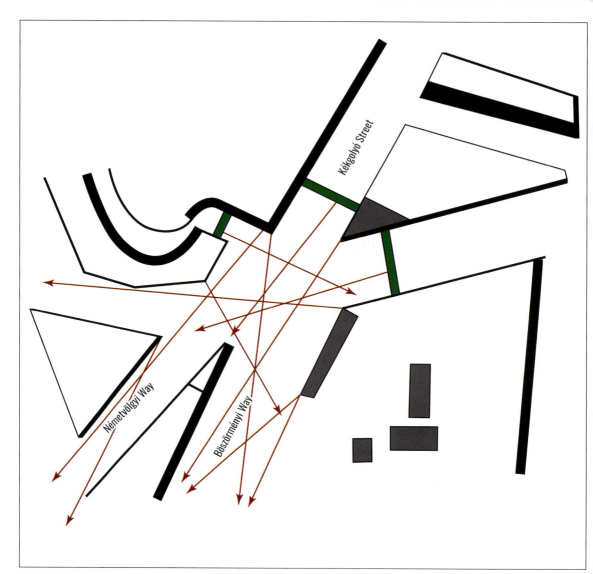

→ Direction of fire

▬ Roadblock

The stronghold set up at the 11. Army Hospital was situated on a commanding height. It controlled simultaneously six streets and in so doing barred access to the Castle District. The solid buildings and the streets blocked by barricades made this stronghold a challenging prospect for the enemy.

Böszörményi Street was covered by firing points in the first buildings of Németvölgyi Street.

A view of one of the buildings of the stronghold.

A barricade blocking Kékgolyó Street. It was under fire from all buildings within the perimeter.

STRONGHOLD 54

Sas-hegy Hill was one of the commanding heights of Buda.

The rocky eastern slope and the houses defending it.

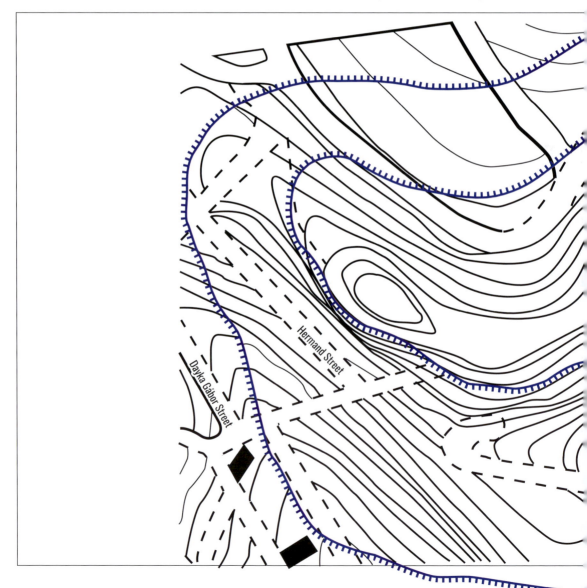

Fortress Budapest | Strongholds

Sas-hegy Hill was one of the commanding heights of Buda. It had open slopes on the south and east, where trenches were dug out, while the western and northern slopes were built up with houses that were very suitable for defence. In so doing, the hill was transformed into a formidable stronghold barring access to the Royal Palace from the south/southwest.
The southern and eastern slopes were protected by two trench lines and the western and northern ones by the houses situated there.

✝ Chapel △ Height
⊥⊥⊥⊥⊥ Trench

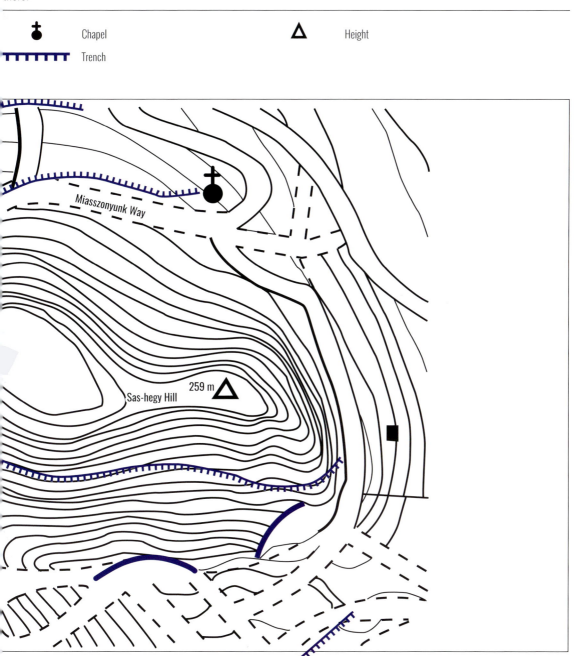

STRONGHOLD 55

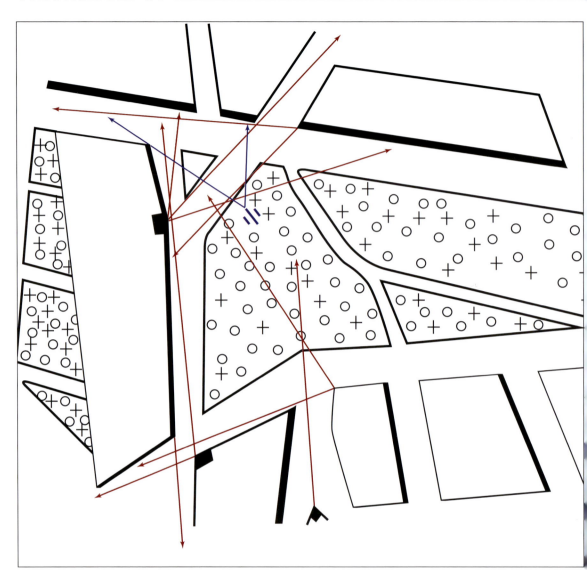

→ Direction of fire

I|I Artillery gun

The stronghold at Németvölgyi Cemetery controlled Gömbös Gyula Way, one of the main avenues of Buda leading to the Castle District. It was reinforced with barricades, an anti-tank ditch and barbed-wire entanglements.

Budaörsi Way. This building was employed for the defence the avenue.

An anti-aircraft artillery position in the vicinity of the stronghold.

A dead-end street. The tall buildings on both sides effectivelly blocked any further advance to downtown Buda.

STRONGHOLD 56

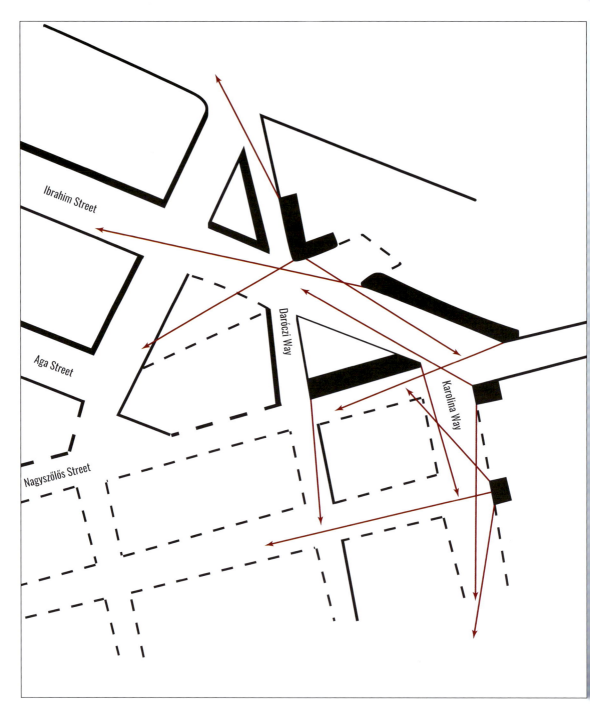

→ Direction of fire

Fortress Budapest | Strongholds

The stronghold at the French-Hungarian cotton factory was made up of buildings and houses that had not been fortified. It controlled the intersection of Bocskai Way, Daróci Way and Karolina Way, and in doing so effectively barred the access to the Citadel. The stronghold was held by the Axis troops for more than ten days.

A broad view of the wide open space in front of the stronghold which was supported by long-range fire from depth positions (mainly from the Citadel.)

A destroyed pocket of resistance in a two-storey house.

STRONGHOLD 57

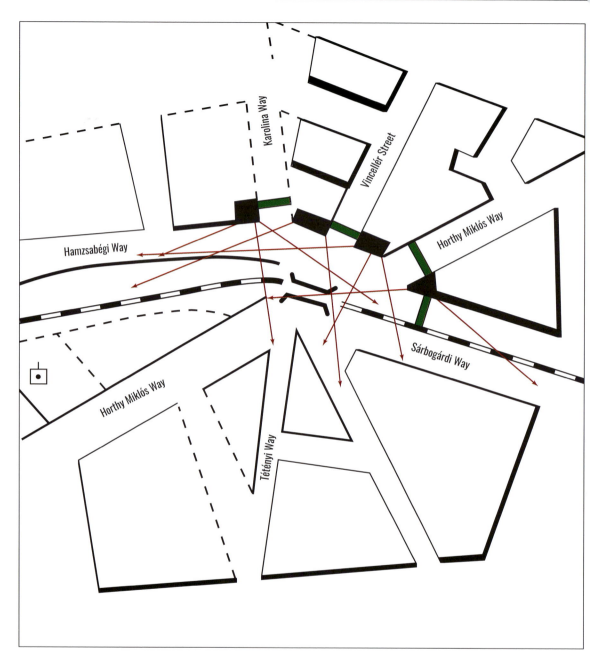
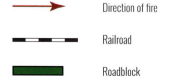

Fortress Budapest | Strongholds

The stronghold at the National Dairy Co-operative Centre protected the approaches to the Castle District from the south/south-west. It was made up of buildings that had not been not fortified. The perimeter was kept under fire from corner buildings, and especially from the windows and loopholes cut in the walls. Barricades were erected on the streets.

A view on Horthy Miklós Way (today Bartók Béla Way). In that sector the avenues were curvilinear, which allowed the defenders to deliver flanking fire from the corner building.

A corner building barring the access to Horthy Miklós Way. It was mostly demolished by the Soviet artillery, but the ground floor and the attic remained intact, which allowed the defenders to continue the fight.

A corner building barring simultaneously the access to Horthy Miklós Way and Karolina Way. The facade had received up to 20 artillery hits, but, nevertheless, it was held by the defenders for nearly ten days.

The intersection of Bocskai Way and Karolina Way.

A four-storey corner building barring simultaneously the access to Hamzsabégi Way, Horthy Miklós Way and Karolina Way.

A corner building barring simultaneously access to Hamzsabégi Way and Vincellér Street. Despite fierce artillery bombardment, it was used by the defenders for a considerable period of time.

A corner building protecting both Bocskai Way and Karolina Way.

A view onto Bocskai Way and the buildings protecting it. They were demolished by the Soviet artillery.

STRONGHOLD 58

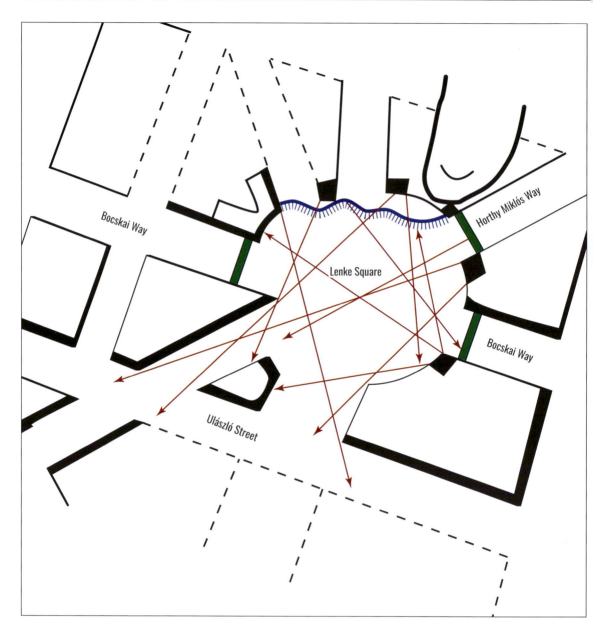

The stronghold at Lenke Square barred access to the Royal Palace and the embankment. It was made up of solid multi-storey buildings adapted for defence by cutting loopholes in their walls. The streets leading to the square, as well as those running from it, were barricaded.

Bocskai Street 31, called Lenke Udvar. The defenders turned the first and second floor into strongpoints with portholes slung into the wall.

STRONGHOLD 59

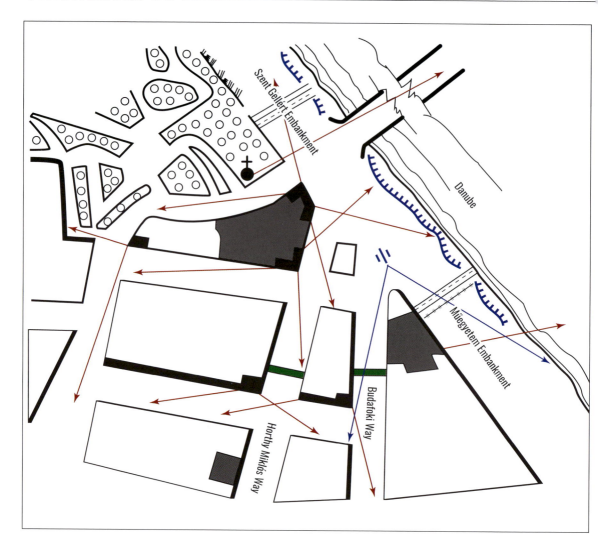

	Direction of fire		Anti-tank ditch		Artillery gun
	Trench		Chapel		
	Roadblock		Barbed wire		

The stronghold at Szent Gellért Square protected the embankment and the near approaches to Ferenc József Bridge. It was made up of buildings adapted for defence, a trench line and barricades. Hotel Gellért formed the core of the stronghold.

Hotel Gellért seen from Kelenvölgyi Street.

The facade of Hotel Gellert.

View of the quay (photographed from Pest).

STRONGHOLD 60

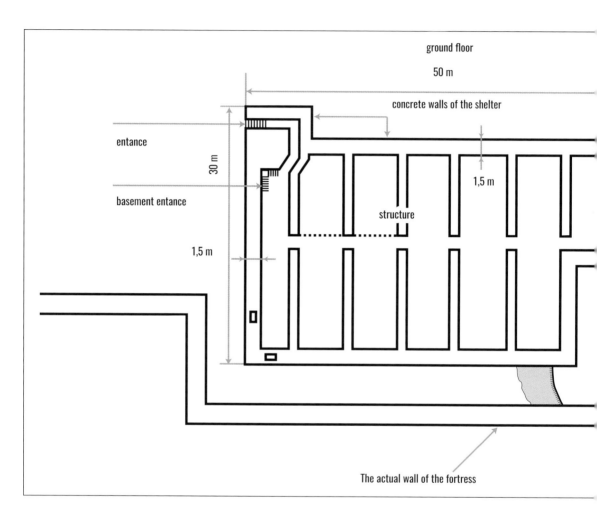

Fortress Budapest | Strongholds

The Citadel had been built on a commanding height and because of this controlled most of the city. To the east, access to the Citadel was limited by the Danube with its steep, rocky riverbank. To the north, west and south there were open passages permitting all-round fire. The thick walls, additionally reinforced before the siege, guaranteed protection for the garrison.

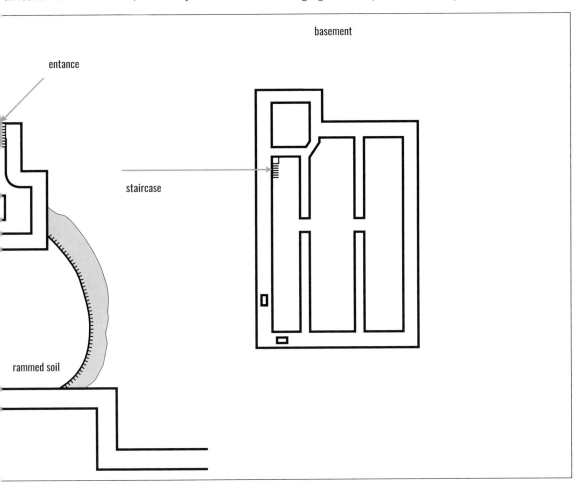

The Citadel (as viewed from Pest across the Danube).

Downtown Pest as viewed from the Citadel (across the Danube).

STRONGHOLD 60

The southern side of the Citadel.

Looking onto the fortress yard.

Fortress Budapest | Strongholds

The southwestern part of the fortress.

STRONGHOLD 60

A demolished part of the Citadel.

The southern side of the Citadel.

Fortress Budapest | Strongholds

Northern part of the fortress.

The Hegedűs-villa barred the access to the Citadel from the north.

The fort in the southern wall of the Citadel. Its loopholes were additionally protected by sandbags.

STRONGHOLD 60

Eastern bridgehead of Ferenc József Bridge (Fővám Square) as seen from Gellért Hill.

Fortress Budapest | Strongholds

Originally planned as command post, during the siege this unfinished bunker was used as an air-raid shelter by the Flak battery positioned in the Citadel.

The commanding height offered excellent observation over most of the city.

STRONGHOLD 61

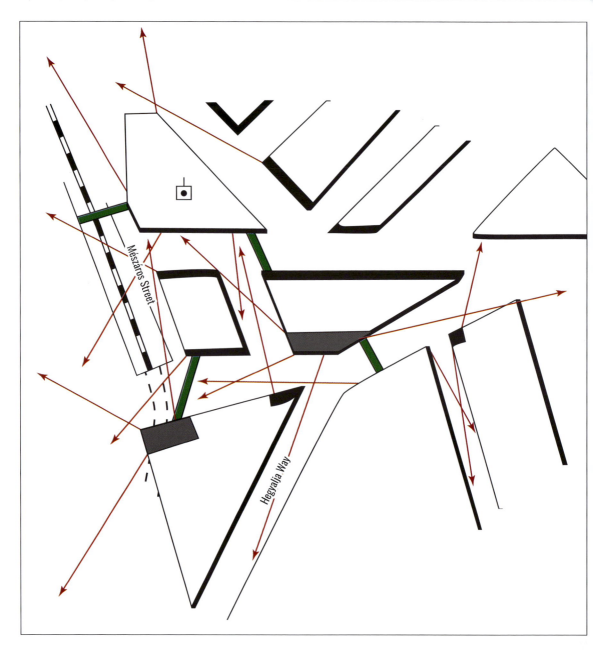

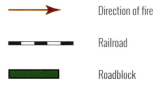

The stronghold at Kis-Gellért-hegy Hill was set up at the intersection of Mészáros Street and Hegyalja Way. It consisted of massive buildings that were not additionally reinforced. The curved streets denied the attackers maneuverability and exposed them to flanking fire.

A barricade on Mészáros Street. A loophole had been cut in the stone fence through which the barricade was defended.

A corner building that kept Hegyalja Way under fire.

STRONGHOLD 62 AND 63

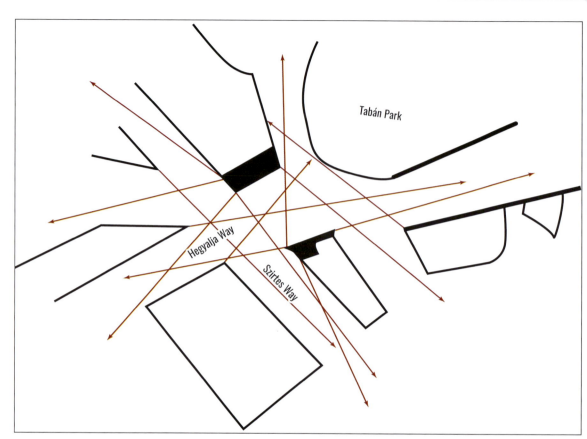

The stronghold at Búsuló Juhász Restaurant controlled simultaneously seven streets and barred the approaches to the Royal Palace. The solid buildings, despite massive aerial and artillery bombardments, were able to withstand the fierce Soviet attacks.

Fortress Budapest | Strongholds

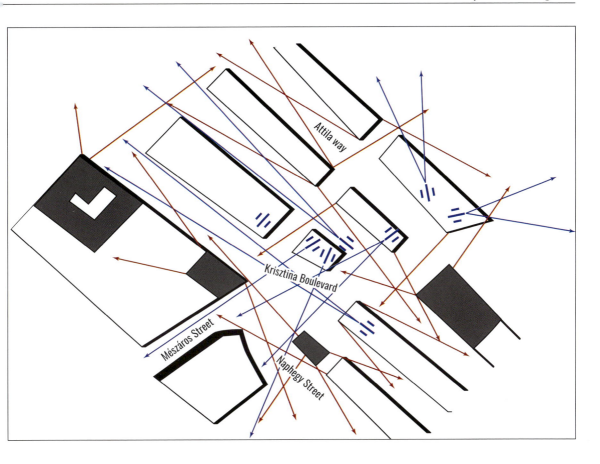

The stronghold at Krisztina Boulevard protected the Royal Place. It simultaneously controlled eight streets. The stronghold consisted of solid stone buildings that withstood massive air raids and artillery bombardments. They were never fully demolished, which allowed the defenders to hold out till the end.

  Direction of fire

  Artillery gun

STRONGHOLD 64

Direction of fire

170

The stronghold at Palota Square protected the near approaches to the Royal Palace. It comprised massive and very solid stone buildings. Furthermore, there was a wide open space in front of it, Tabán Park. Not surprisingly, it was held by the defenders till the very end. The Royal Palace, which had been built on a commanding height, formed the core of the stronghold and controlled most of Buda. The palace, with its high fence and open space to the south of it (Tabán Park), was a natural fortress.

This corner building on Palota Square survived the heavy artillery bombardment.

This building, heavily damaged by the airforce, was occupied by the defenders till the very end of the battle.

The supporting wall of the Royal Pallace was used both as an anti-personnel and anti-tank obstacle.

The supporting wall of the Royal Pallace was used both as an anti-personnel and anti-tank obstacle.

STRONGHOLD 64

The Royal Palace seen from Váralja Street. Today there is a sports court on the site of the building seen on the left.

Northwest corner of Palota Square and Szent János Square.

Statue of Horse Drawn Artillery on Palota Square (today: Dózsa György Square).

The statue from a different angle.

STRONGHOLD 65

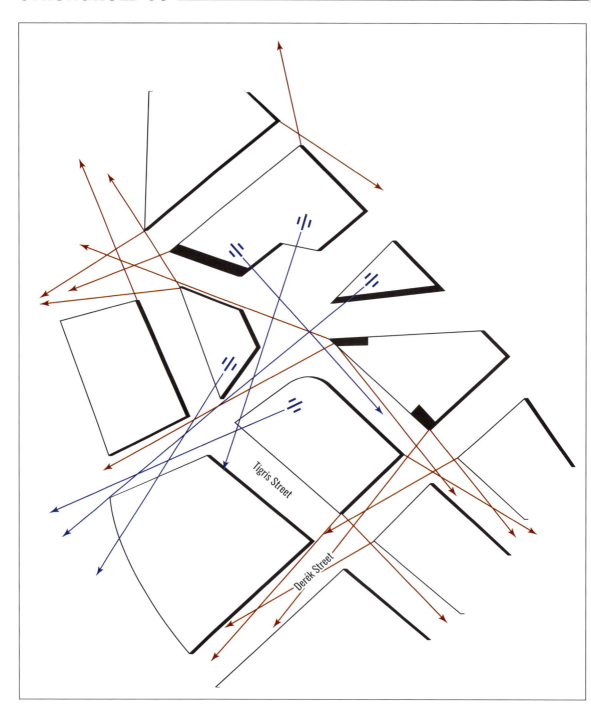

 Direction of fire

Artillery gun

The stronghold at Naphegy Square protected the near approaches to the Royal Palace. It was made of massive stone buildings that withstood many aerial and artillery bombardments.

The corner of Fenyő Street and Párduc Street at Tigris Street.

STRONGHOLD 66

Direction of fire

Chapel

The Royal Palace and the government buildings surrounding it formed a stronghold that was literally the garrison's last line of defence. The palace, which had been built on a commanding height, had a number of underground tunnels and bunkers that facilitated the efforts of the defenders to a considerable degree.

A view of the southern and eastern side of the palace.

A view over the Danube from the top of the palace.

A view of the palace.

The once beautiful dome of the palace suffered severe damage.

STRONGHOLD 66

Loopholes in the main facade of the palace.

A view of the main facade of the palace with the remains of the dome in the background.

An artillery position at the Fisherman's Bastion.

A view of the Fisherman's Bastion.

Fortress Budapest | Strongholds

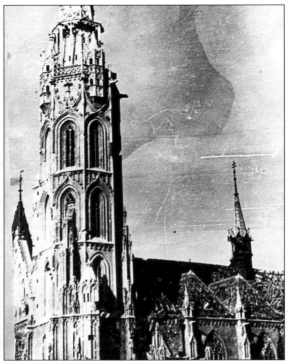

Matthias Church allowed unobstructed observation in all directions.

The damaged Fisherman's Bastion.

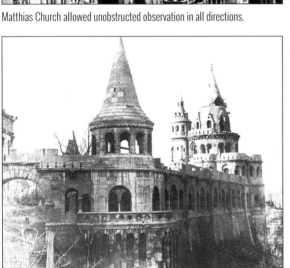

A view on the Fisherman's Bastion. It has since been restored to its former glory.

The ruined building of the Royal Barn.

STRONGHOLD 66

The palace yard was defended from the windows and from the dome.

The Royal Palace was built on a commanding height, overlooking the entire Castle District. In so doing it controlled the adjacent square.

Archduke Joseph Palace could be reached only through stairs that were easy to protect and defend.

Flak 36/37 anti-aircraft gun built on VOMAG bus chassis on the promenade north of the Fisherman's Bastion. (The promenade doesn't exists today, Hotel Budapest Hilton is in its place).

STRONGHOLD 66

A view of garrison's last line of defence - the Royal Palace, the Ministry of Defence and Archduke Joseph Palace.

The supporting wall of Archduke Joseph Palace was 6 m high. It served as an anti-personnel obstacle.

The supporting wall of the Royal Palace along Palota Way was 6 m high. The approaches to the wall were kept under fire from the palace.

The narrow streets in the vicinity of the castle facilitated the defence, while the thick walls offered protection for the equipment.

STRONGHOLD 67

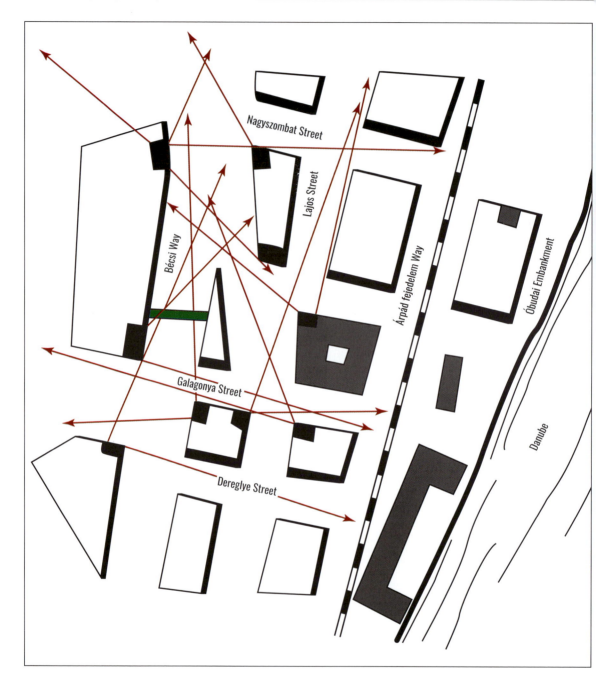

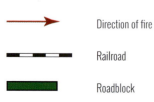

Stronghold 67 at Kolosy Square barred the access to Bécsi Way and Lajos Street, thereby protecting the northern approaches to the Castle District. It was made up of multi-storey residential buildings, barricades and anti-tank ditches.

This corner building on Bécsi Way had received up to 20 direct artillery hits.

STRONGHOLD 68

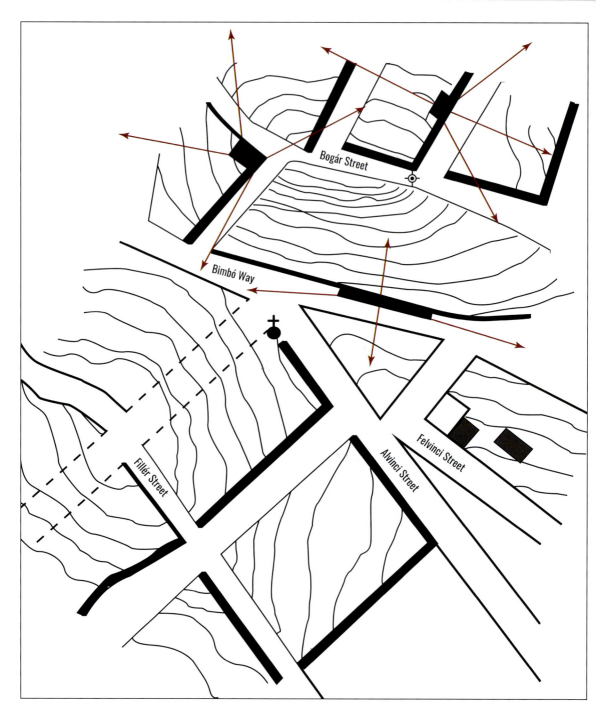

Direction of fire

Chapel

Rókus-hegy Hill, one of the commanding heights overlooking the Buda bridgehead, protected the avenues leading to the downtown parts of Budapest. The stronghold set up there was made of multi-storey residential buildings. It had excellent fields of fire, because the built-up sectors alternated with vacant land. This allowed the defenders to hold this position for a long period of time.

One of the solid four-storey residential buildings protecting the hill.

FORTRESS BUDAPEST
SKETCHES

SKETCHES

The machine gun fire system of the northwestern edge of Castle Hill towards Vérmező

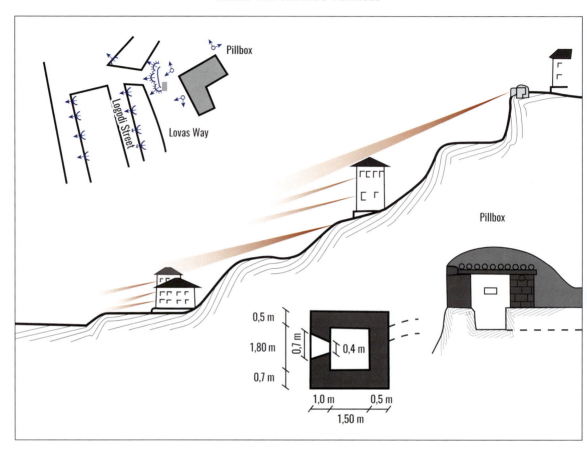

Machine gun

Light machine gun

The capture of Erzsébet Salt Baths building at the corner of Szent Korona Way and Tétényi Way on 1 Jan 1945

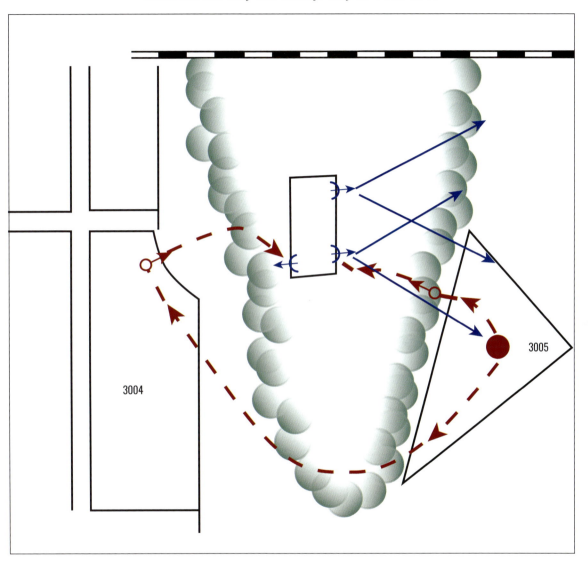

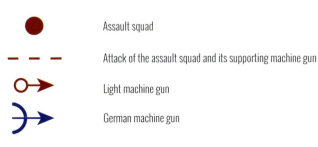

SKETCHES

Anti-tank ditch system at the corner of Némedvölgyi Way and Orbánhegyi Way

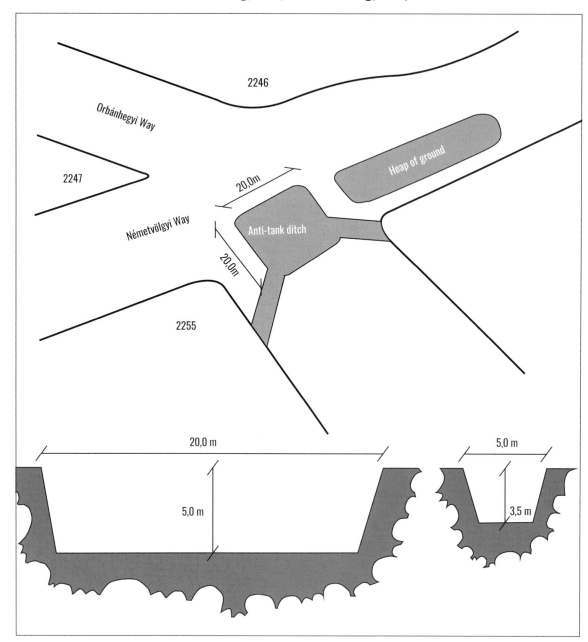

Fortress Budapest

The defence system of South Railroad Station's region

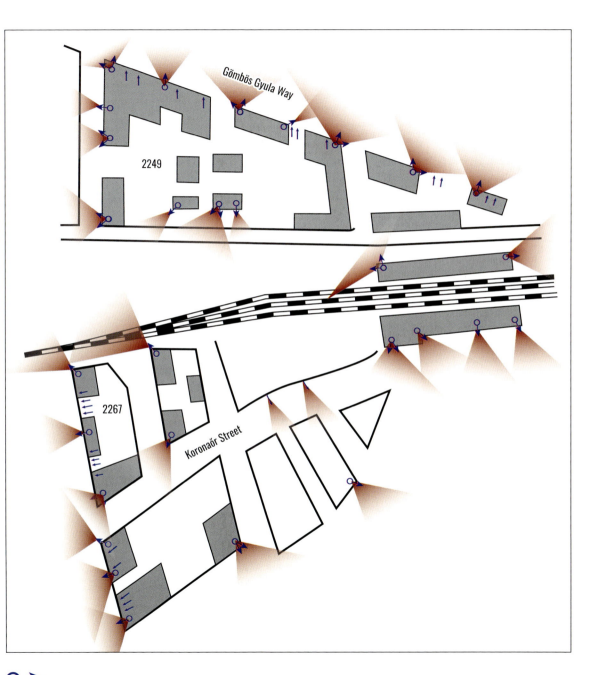

 Light machine gun

→ Rifleman

SKETCHES

The German-Hungarian defence system in the vicinity of the University of Technology

Artillery pillbox on the embankment near the University of Technology

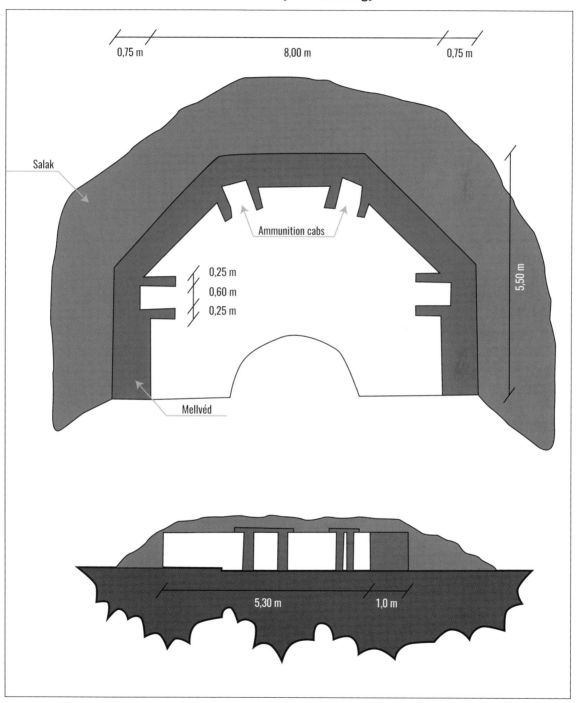

SKETCHES

Assault by elements of the Soviet 312th Guards Rifle Regiment on Block 616 at the corner of Zápor Street and Selmeci Street on 22 Jan 1945

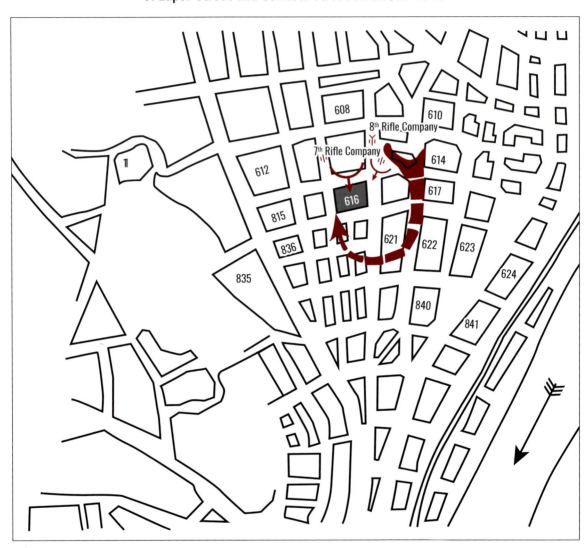

Artillery gun

Anti-tank gun

Fortress Budapest

The combat action of 109th Guards Rifle Division's assault groups along Lajos Street on 22/23 Jan 1945

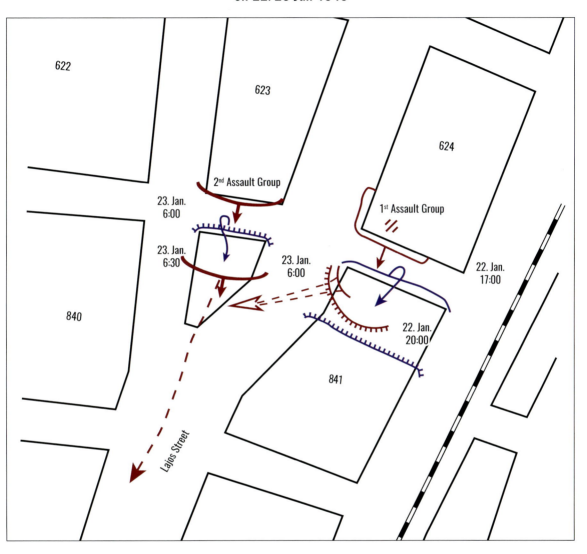

Artillery gun

German-Hungarian position

Soviet position

SKETCHES

The capture of a building in the Olasz Alley with flamethrowers on 25 Jan 1945

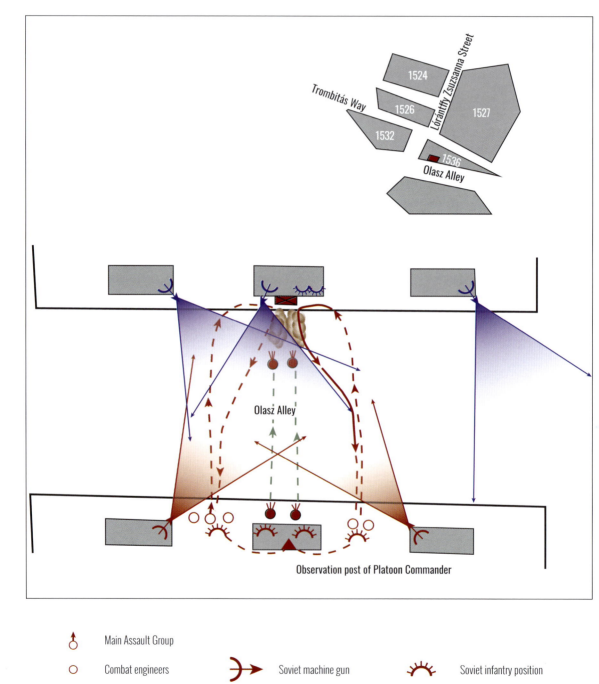

The advance of the 320th Rifle Division towards downtown Buda was checked in the vicinity of the lower terminus of the cogwheel railway by determined Axis resistance. There the defenders had set up a solid strongpoint in the three-storey building containing the luxurious Café "Rajna Park". The direct attack launched by the Soviet infantry failed and the decision was made to take it by assault group.

The assault group was made of 6 riflemen, 6 sappers and 2 flamethrower operators. It was armed with six 12 kg charges, six detonators, twelve hand grenades, six submachine guns, four rifles and two flamethrowers. Two heavy Maxim machine guns provided fire cover for the group. The assignment was to blow up the building and torch the garrison with flamethrowers.

The group was assembled in the lower terminus of the cogwheel railway where it was briefed in detail by its commander. The commanders of both subgroups - the blocking subgroup and the fire-cover subgroup - discussed their cooperation.

At 22:00 the blocking group surged forward. The sappers carried with them the explosive charges. Having split into two three-men teams, they began to outflank the building to the left and right, respectively. But the garrison of the building, who repeatedly illuminated the perimeter with flares, spotted them and opened murderous fire.

In response, the commander of the fire-cover subgroup ordered both Maxim machine guns to open fire on the building. But despite their assistance and protection, it was only at 24:00 that the sappers succeeded in reaching the café.

At the café, two of the sappers placed the explosive charges, while the other two set up the detonators. Then all of them stepped back. The charges were finally ignited from a distance and the building was demolished.

Immediately after the explosion both flamethrower operators rushed across the street and set the building on fire. The blocking group that followed closely behind them threw hand grenades through the window openings and then entered the café. A total of 11 dead bodies were counted inside. The successful action of the assault group allowed the division to secure the entire block.

SKETCHES

The capture of Block 844 at the corner of Lajos Street and Galagonya Street on 27 Jan 1945

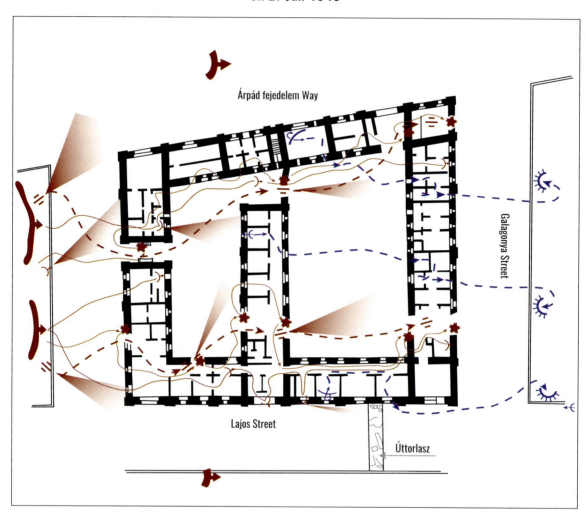

 The attack of assault group (including riflemen and demolition specialists)

 Demolitions for crossing the walls

 The movement of regimental artillery gun

Fortress Budapest

The attack of 305th Guards Rifle Regiment assault group on 30 Jan 1945

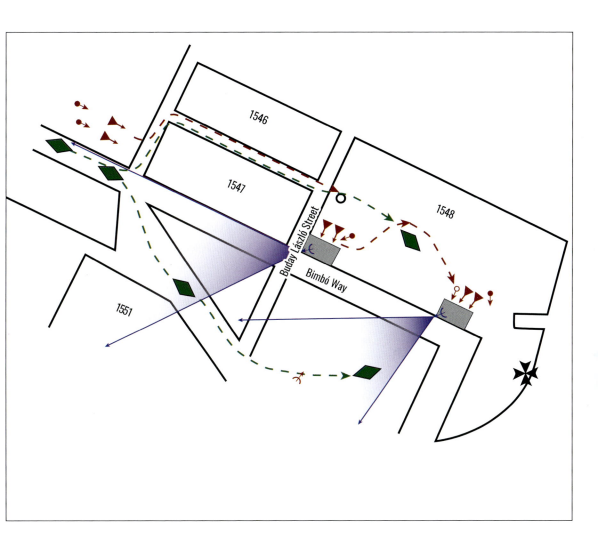

Blocking combat engineer

Tank support for blocking force

Submachine gunner for covering fire

Light machine gun of 305th GRR for covering fire

Fortified building of German defenders

Five riflemen of 305th GRR and the commander of assault group

SKETCHES

Attack of Soviet assault group against a building in the block of Nárcisz Street, Vöröskő Street and Gyimesi Street on 2 Feb 1945

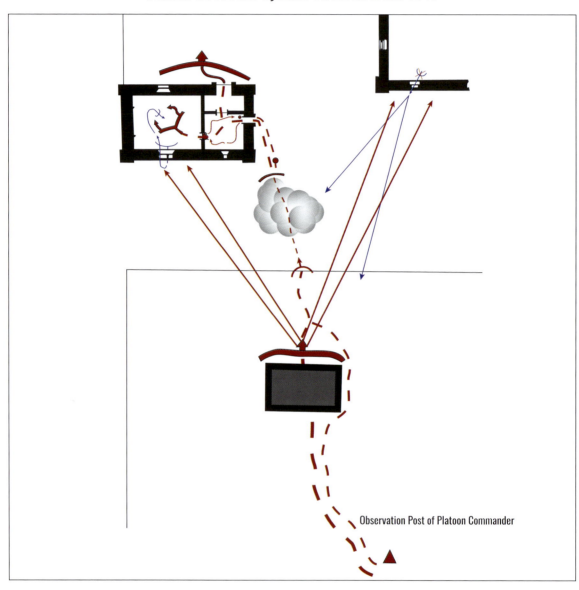

Assault combat engineers

Covering group

Smoke for hiding

German-Hungarian fire position

Fortress Budapest

The German-Hungarian defence system of King Károly (now Petőfi) Barracks

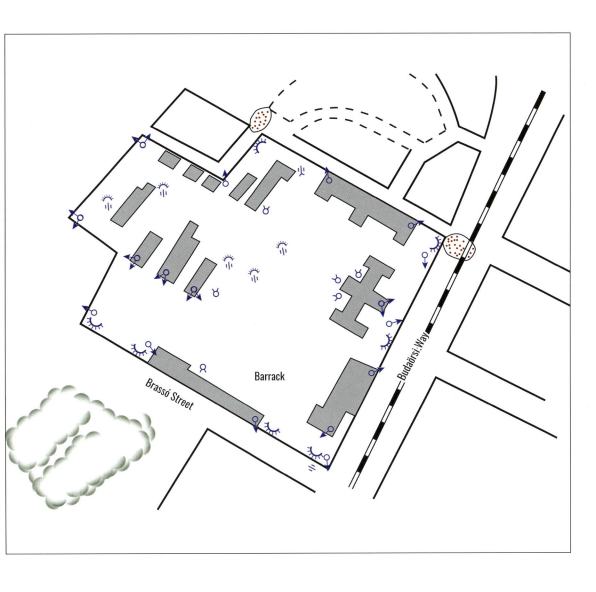

	Minefield		Light machine guns in pairs
	Anti-tank gun		Artillery gun
	Light machine gun		Mortar

SKETCHES

The capture of Block 2260 on 5 Feb 1945

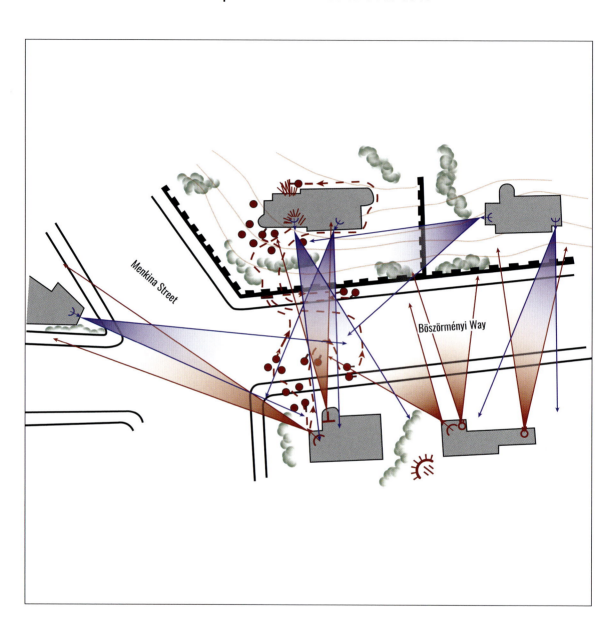

Following the loss of Sas-hegy Hill, the Axis troops hurriedly began to strengthen the perimeter to the southeast of it. Some of the buildings there were very well suited for the purpose. They had been erected on hills or on hill slopes, were 4 to 6-stories high and had basements. Furthermore, they were surrounded by metal or brick fences that were 0.5 - 0.8 m thick and 1.5 - 2 m high.

One of those buildings was the 5-storey house on 38 Böszörményi Way, not far from the gendarme barracks. It was surrounded by a brick fence that was about 1.8 m high and 0.8 m thick. On each of the second and third floors there was a machine gun. Two snipers had taken positions on the fifth floor, while the basement was occupied by a group of infantrymen. (Soviet intelligence reports show that the area was defended by elements of SS-Cavalry Regiments 17 and 18 additionally reinforced with some Hungarian troops.)

The task of taking the building was assigned to an assault group formed by the 311th Guards Rifle Regiment (of the 108th Guards Rifle Division). It consisted of 6 infantrymen and 3 combat engineers. They were supported by one 45-mm AT gun, one heavy machine gun and one AT rifle.

On 5 February the assault group assembled in a small house across the street. Right from the outset it was clear that taking the strongpoint by direct attack was out of question - all of the approaches to it were under intense machine gun fire. The commander of the group therefore decided to storm the building after sunset. The plan was to blow passages in the brick fence and then, as morning approached, to attack the strongpoint at once.

At 24:00 two engineers carrying a 20 kg explosive charge advanced toward the building but, in the middle of the street, were illuminated by a flare and pinned down by murderous machine gun fire. It was 04:00 when both men finally succeeded in reaching the fence. Then they placed the explosive charge and prepared it for detonation, waiting for a signal from their commander.

The go-ahead order came at 06:00. The fuse was ignited and the powerful explosion tore down part of the fence. The rest of the assault group immediately rushed through the newly-opened passage. During the dash it was effectively protected by the assigned heavy weapons, which fired relentlessly on the Axis firing points. The fire support worked well and before long all members of the group reached the walls of the building. Then they quickly outflanked it and attacked simultaneously from two directions. Two of the infantrymen threw grenades into the room where a machine gun had been installed. In the meantime, another infantryman blew up the front door with an anti-tank grenade and jumped inside. The rest of the group followed him. In the ensuing brief battle 7 Axis soldiers and 1 officer were killed, while two others were taken prisoner. Thus by the morning of 6 February the entire block had fallen into Soviet hands.

SKETCHES

The capture of the group of buildings at the corner of Fürj Street and Sirály Street on 6 Feb 1945

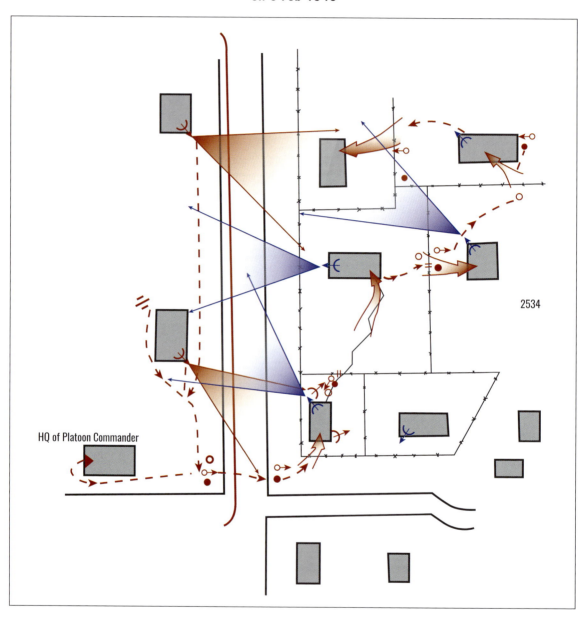

The Soviet 320th Rifle Division fought a very difficult battle between Sashegy Hill and the Németvölgyi Cemetery. Cleverly using the features of the terrain (the low elevation of the hill), the Axis defenders offered fierce resistance. They were further aided by the fact that the area was sparsely built, on which offered an excellent field of fire and the possibility for close cooperation between the strongpoints. Moreover, trenches were dug out around some of the houses.

The stronghold set up in the block framed by Wolff Károly Way, Fürj Street, Vércse Street and Somorjai Street played an especially important role in the plans of the defenders because it protected the distant approaches to the Castle Hill. The Soviets knew that as well and put a lot of effort into taking it.

The direct attacks of the infantrymen of the 320th Rifle Divisions were beaten back by machine guns positioned in the western sides of the houses. Then the Soviet commanders assembled a dedicated assault group for the task of capturing the building. Taking into account that the houses occupied by the Axis troops were surrounded by a massive fence, the Soviet commander reinforced the group with combat engineers whose assignment was to blow passages in the fence.

The group consisted of 6 infantrymen (submachine gunners), 2 assault engineers and 1 flamethrower operator. Apart from the submachine guns, they were armed with 24 high-explosive hand grenades, 24 anti-tank hand grenades, two explosive charges (6 and 8 kg, respectively) and two barbed-wire cutters. The fire cover and support was provided by two heavy 7.62-mm Maxim machine guns and one 45-mm AT gun.

The group assembled in one of the empty houses of the neighboring block. From there the enemy positions and the approaches to them could be observed. In the meantime, the fire-cover sub-group moved into position in the two houses situated to the north of the house occupied by the assault group. The mission of the latter was, by opening a very intense fire on the houses on the other side of the street, to divert the attention of the Axis troops garrisoning them from the movements of the assault group.

Having dressed themselves in white camouflage clothes, the Soviet assault troops quickly crossed the street. As was expected, the Axis defenders failed to spot them because their attention was preoccupied with the Maxim machine guns firing on them. This allowed the group to assemble in front of the barbed wire obstacles. Then the combat engineers, skillfully using cutters, succeeded in opening passages in the barbed wire obstacles in a matter of five minutes.

The first objective of the group was the house on the street corner. One of the submachine gunners approached it from the south and threw two hand grenades through the window openings. As result of the explosions, two German troops were killed and the machine gunner was wounded. The rest of the German garrison panicked and took cover in the basement. Determined to finish them off, the Soviets immediately threw in their four anti-tank grenades. Before long it turned out that the grenades had destroyed most of the occupants, while the five Germans who survived the attack had no choice left but to surrender. Once the house was completely secured, both Maxim machine guns were moved closer to the assault troops.

From that moment on the assault group acted like a spearhead for the rest of the company. The engineers blew passages in the fences and blocked the houses, thus allowing the friendly infantry to secure them completely. Before long four more houses were seized and thus on 6 February the entire block fell into Soviet hands.

SKETCHES

The German-Hungarian defence system in the vicinity of Farkasréti Cemetery

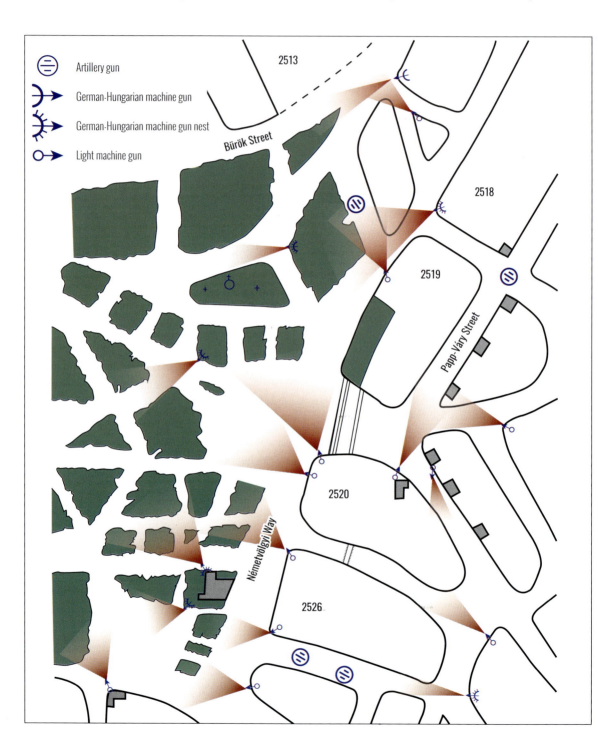

Fortress Budapest

The German-Hungarian defence system in the area around Apáthy Rock (258 m)

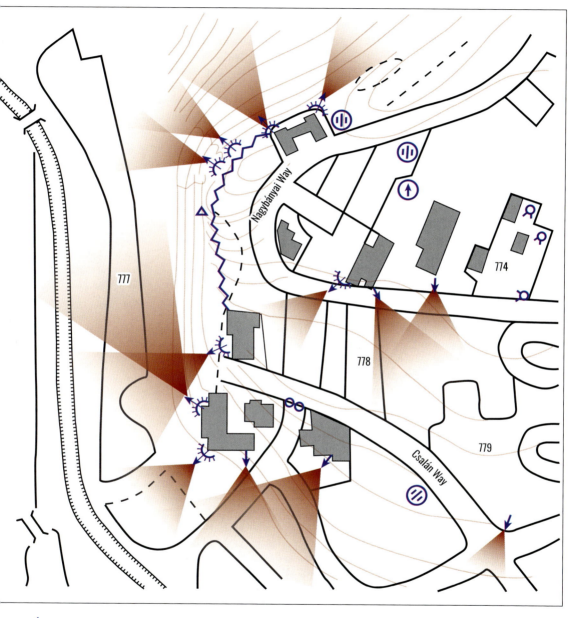

 German-Hungarian machine gun nest Mortar

 Light machine gun Observation post

 Artillery gun Anti-aircraft gun

SKETCHES

The German-Hungarian defence system of Bimbó Way and Törökvész Way

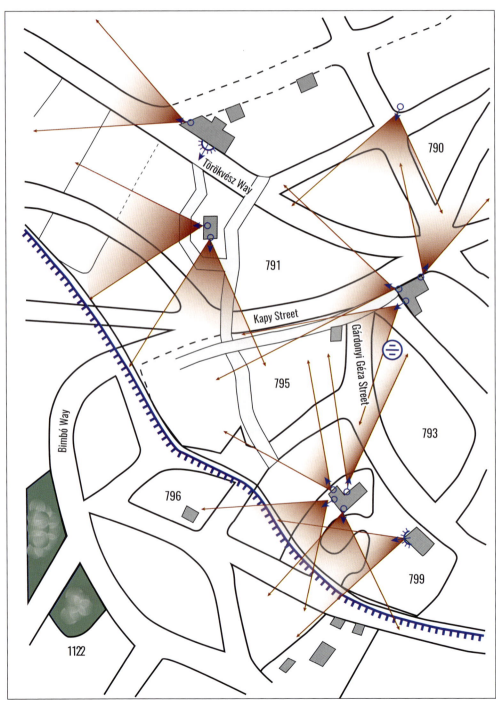

 German-Hungarian machine gun nest Light machine gun   Artillery gun Mortar

Fortress Budapest

The German-Hungarian defence system around the Royal Hungarian Vineyard and Vine Institute block on Hermann Ottó Way

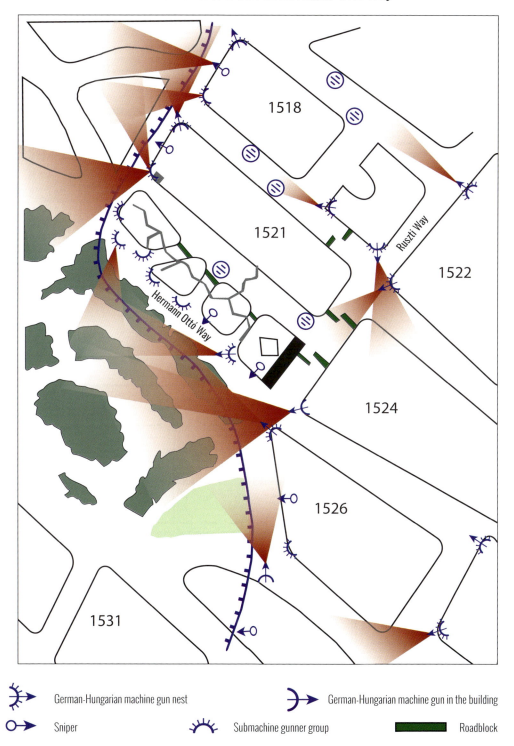

SKETCHES

The assault into the three-floor building of Hermann Ottó Way No. 15

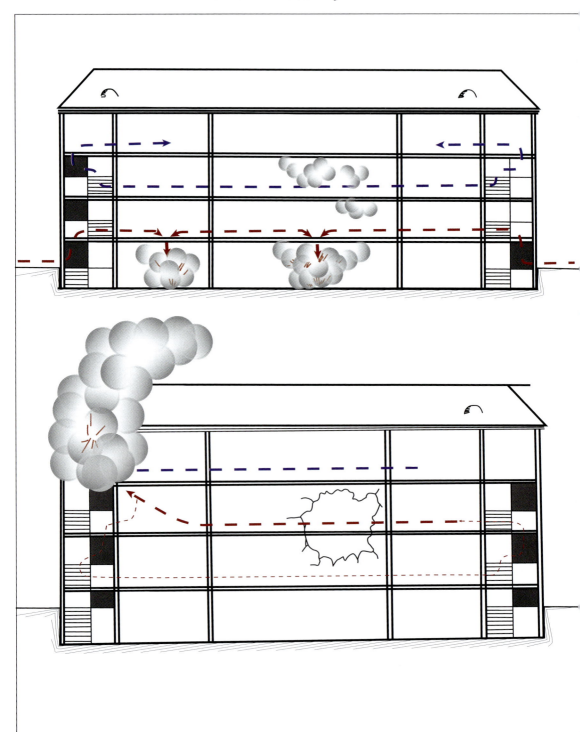

The three-storey building at 15 Herman Ottó Way (the Institute of Viniculture) had been turned into an important stronghold that protected the approaches to two other blocks that were also controlled by the Axis troops. The building itself was very solid and its basement was capable of withstanding direct hits by 76-mm rounds.

The leadership of the Soviet 311th Guards Rifle Regiment created a dedicated assault group with the sole mission of taking the institute. It succeeded in penetrating into the first floor, but was "showered" with hand grenades from above (through special ports cut by the defenders in the upper flour) and was forced to withdraw.

A new group was formed, which had the following composition:

12 infantrymen
8 assault engineers
2 flamethrower operators

The group was armed with 20 submachine guns, 2 backpack flamethrowers, 40 fragmentation hand grenades and 12 anti-tank grenades. The engineers also carried with them six 8 kg explosive charges and four 12 kg explosive charges. The group was supported by two 7.62-mm Maxim heavy machine guns and one 45-mm AT gun.

The attack was preceded by a short, but intense artillery bombardment delivered by the artillery available to the 3rd Battalion of the 311th Guards Rifle Regiment. Then the group, effectively protected by the two Maxims, dashed to the building. The Axis defenders fired back relentlessly with all weapons at their disposal, but it was too late – the group had already reached the building. Having thrown several hand grenades through the window openings, the Soviets broke inside.

The small Axis garrison reacted immediately and began throwing grenades from the second floor, The Soviet assault troops, however, had expected that and approached very carefully.

On the floor they noticed the same ports, which had been made by the defenders to allow them to throw grenades into the basement. The group commander decided to use the ports to destroy the Axis troops below him. Then the engineers ignited the fuses and threw two 8-kg charges through the ports. Most of the defenders were killed instantly, the rest were shocked by the explosions.

Then the Soviet assault group turned its attention to the second floor. They placed two 12-kg explosives just below the window openings, near the portholes in the floor, and ignited the fuses. As result of the powerful explosions, the entire wall collapsed. Exploiting the confusion among the defenders, the assault group immediately stormed the second floor and quickly secured it. Their attempt to move to the third floor, however, was beaten back by the Axis troops still occupying it.

The commander of the assault ordered the engineers to place the remaining two 12-kg explosive charges in the ceiling. The ensuing explosion caused one of the upper corners of the building to collapse. The Soviets immediately entered the third floor through the breach, encountering no resistance in the process. They found there two machine guns and seven dead bodies of German soldiers. The remainder of the garrison (five German troops) surrendered. Thus the Institute of Viniculture finally fell into Soviet hands. The defenders lost 18 killed and 5 captured; the losses of the attackers amounted to just three wounded.

SKETCHES

The German-Hungarian defence system of Kis-Sváb-hegy Hill (259 m)

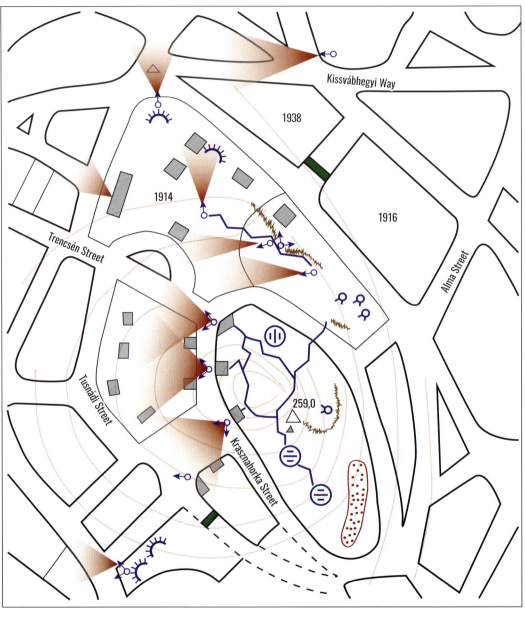

Fortress Budapest

The German-Hungarian defence system of Ministry of Defence area in the Castle

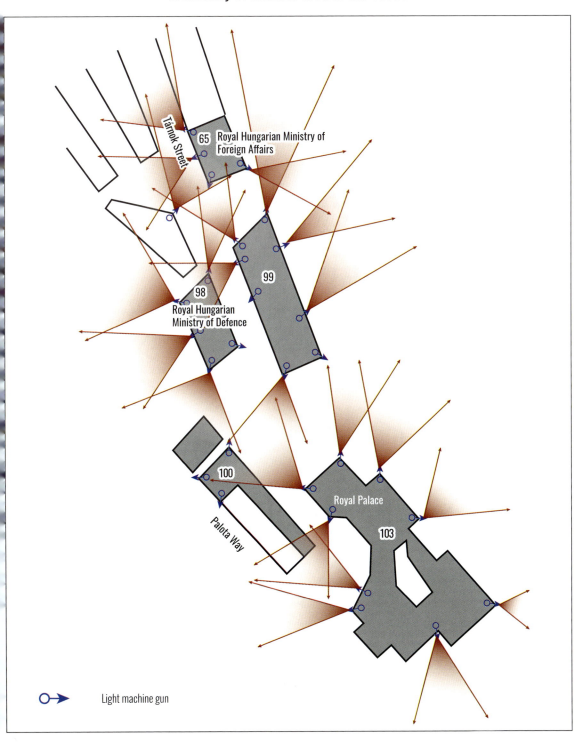

SKETCHES

The defence system of the Royal Palace

 Light machine gun

Light machine guns in pair

Roadblock

 Artillery gun

The fire-support system of Citadel on Gellérthegy Hill (Object No. 128)

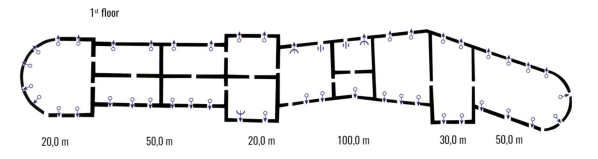

1st floor

20,0 m 50,0 m 20,0 m 100,0 m 30,0 m 50,0 m

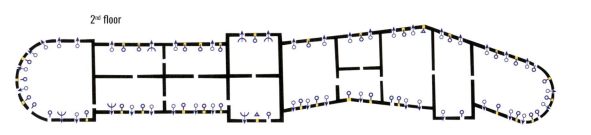

2nd floor

The walls are 1,25-1,90 m thick, the size of the windows is 0,60x0,70 m.

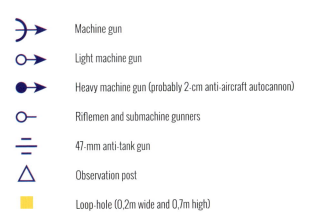

Machine gun

Light machine gun

Heavy machine gun (probably 2-cm anti-aircraft autocannon)

Riflemen and submachine gunners

47-mm anti-tank gun

Observation post

Loop-hole (0,2m wide and 0,7m high)

SKETCHES

The German-Hungarian defence system of Sas-hegy Hill

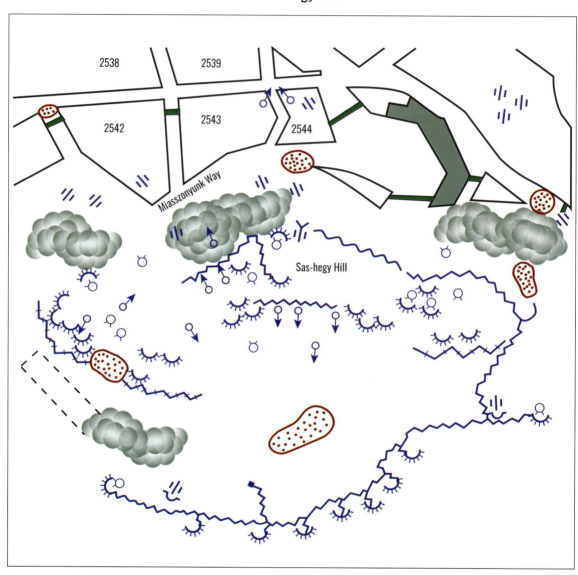

Solid pillbox in the ditch of a road on a hillside

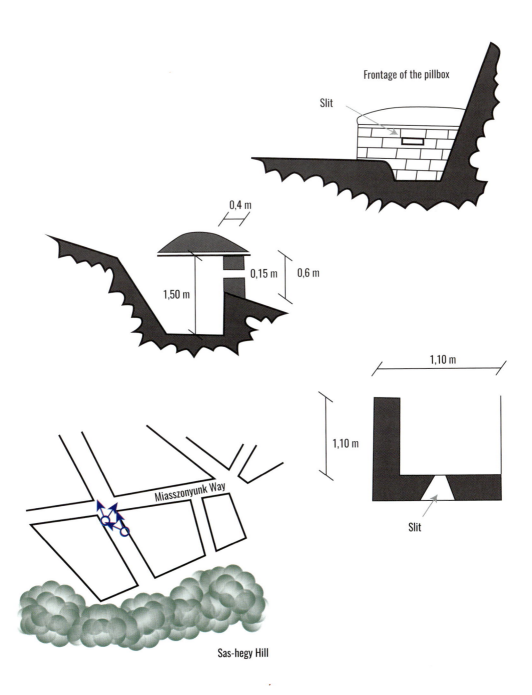

SKETCHES

Concrete machine gun nest

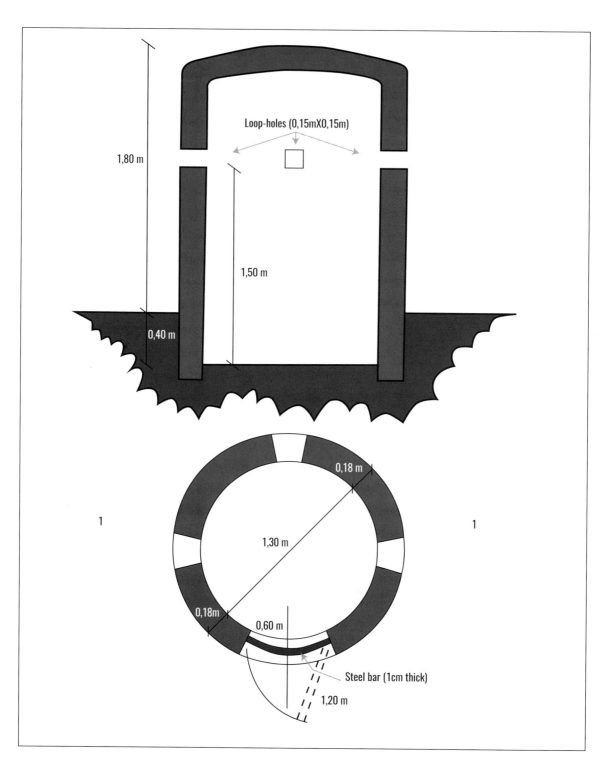

Machine gun nest on Pusztaszeri Way

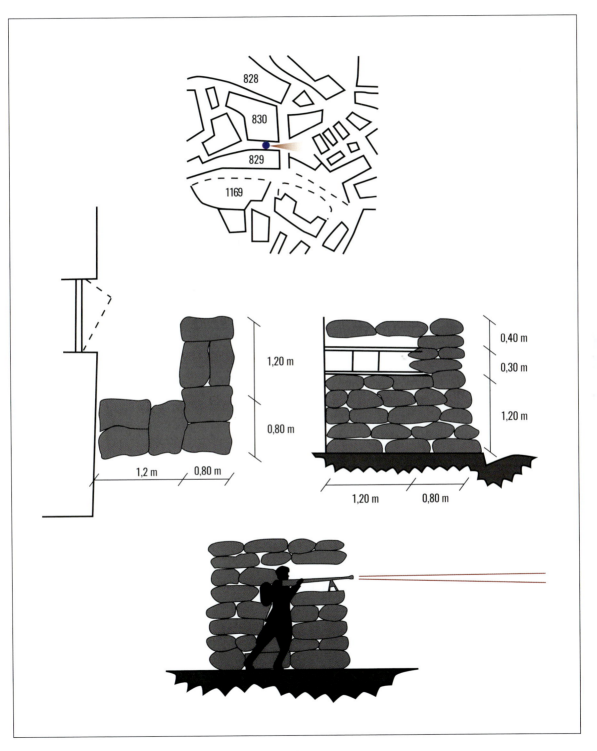

SKETCHES

Firing position for submachine gunner

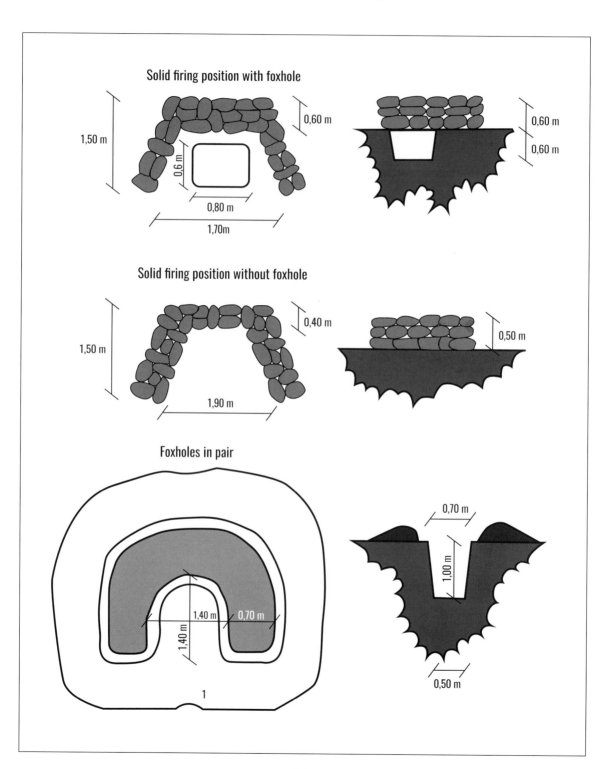

Machine gun nest on Attila Way

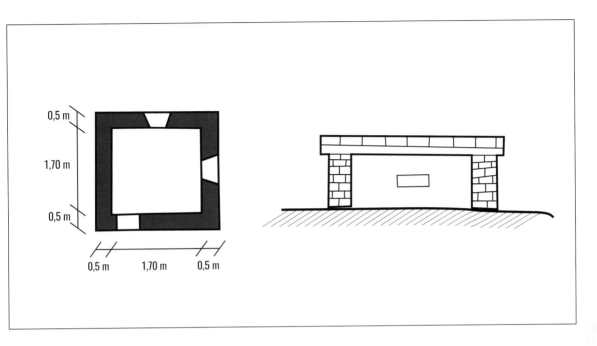

Solid foxhole on the embankment

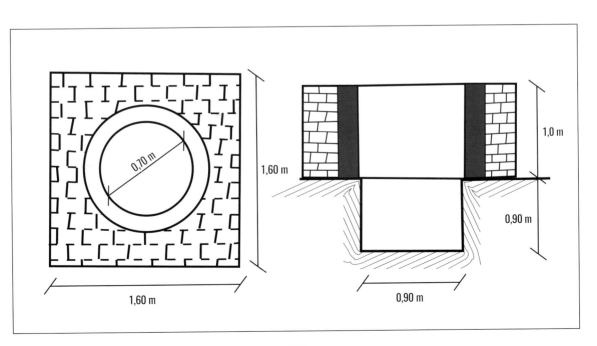

FORTRESS BUDAPEST
PHOTOS

PRELUDE

The western bridgehead of Erzsébet Bridge before the siege.

Anti-tank ditch and "dragon's teeth" around Mogyoród.

"Dragon's teeth" near Fót.

Trench system at Hill 168.

PRELUDE

Barbed wire obstacles at Árpádföld.

Trenches at Hill 168.

Anti-tank ditch and vertically dug-in rails around Csömör.

Barbed wire obstacles at Hill 133.

PRELUDE

Coloumn of whitewashed SU-76M assault guns waiting to be transferred to the western bank of the Danube.

Pz.Kpfw. V Panther Ausf. A, west of Buda. This vehicle belonged to one of the two Panzer-Divisions encircled in the capital.

German soldiers inspecting an abandoned T-34/85 of the 2nd Guards Mechanized Corps outside of Pest.

Destroyed T-34/76 of 13th Guards Mechanized Brigade of 4th Guards Mechanized Corps somewhere East of Pest.

PRELUDE

PaK 40 anti-tank gun.

M1937 152-mm ML-20 howitzer-gun of 17th Guards Cannon-Artillery Brigade on the outskirts of Pest.

Soviet T-34/85 with infantry outside Budapest.

T-34/85 of the 5th Guards Tank Corps.

FIGHTS IN THE CITY

Colonel-General Beregfy inspecting the trenches of 17. SS-Kavallerie-Regiment in the "Attila" line in November 1944. The German officer beside him is SS-Sturmbannführer Karl-Heinz Keitel.

SS-troops at the New Szent János Hospital.

An SS-soldier in a trench outside of Budapest.

15-cm Hummel self-propelled gun of "Feldherrnhalle" Panzer-Division at Szarvas Square.

FIGHTS IN THE CITY

SS-troops with a PaK 40 anti-tank gun.

T-34/85 at the Rákosrendező railyard.

Attacking Soviet soldiers at the railyard.

Soviet scout at Kálvária Square.

FIGHTS IN THE CITY

Soviet ML-20 152-mm howitzer-gun on Kálvária Square.

Soviet ML-20 152-mm howitzer-gun on Kálvária Square.

Soviet 122-mm howitzers.

B-4 203-mm howitzer of the 109th Guards Super-Heavy Artillery Brigade.

FIGHTS IN THE CITY

B-4 203-mm howitzer of the 109th Guards Super-Heavy Artillery Brigade.

B-4 203-mm howitzer of the 109th Guards Super-Heavy Artillery Brigade.

B-4 203-mm howitzer of the 109th Guards Super-Heavy Artillery Brigade.

B-4 203-mm howitzer of the 109th Guards Super-Heavy Artillery Brigade.

FIGHTS IN THE CITY

109th Guards Super-Heavy Artillery Brigade crossing the Danube.

109th Guards Super-Heavy Artillery Brigade crossing the Danube.

Soviet riflemen at the Királyi Serfőzde (Royal Brewery) at Kőbánya.

Soviet troops on Kossuth Lajos Street.

FIGHTS IN THE CITY

Soviet radio oprators on Kálvin Square.

Clearing the rubble.

Soviet "Katyusha" rocket-launcher in front of Szent László Catholic Church in Kőbánya.

ZiS-3 76,2-mm gun of 66th Guards Rifle Division in the Üllői Way, next to the Museum of Applied Arts.

FIGHTS IN THE CITY

SU-76M self-propelled guns of 72nd Guards Self-Propelled Artillery Battalion (68th Guards Rifle Division) turning into Üllői Way from Telepy Street.

SU-76M self-propelled gun of 72nd Guards Self-Propelled Artillery Battalion (68th Guards Rifle Division) turning into Üllői Way from Telepy Street.

SU-76M self-propelled gun of 72nd Guards Self-Propelled Artillery Battalion (68th Guards Rifle Division) turning into Üllői Way from Telepy Street.

Romanian anti-tank gun in Pest.

FIGHTS IN THE CITY

Soviet troops on Üllői Way at the Márton Street.

Soviet 122-mm howitzer at the eastern bridgehead of Erzsébet Bridge.

Soviet artillery at the outskirts of Budapest.

Soviet anti-aircraft artillery on József Boulevard, at Pál Street.

FIGHTS IN THE CITY

Street fights in Buda.

Soviet riflemen in Buda.

Soviet troops covering POWs as they emerge from a cellar.

Soviet riflemen during street fights.

FIGHTS IN THE CITY

Soviet 122-mm howitzer during the street fights in Buda.

Soviet flamethrower troops at the corner of Böszörményi Way - Királyhágó Street.

Soviet troops with captured Hungarian flags.

Milós Steinmetz on a bier.

AERIAL PHOTOS

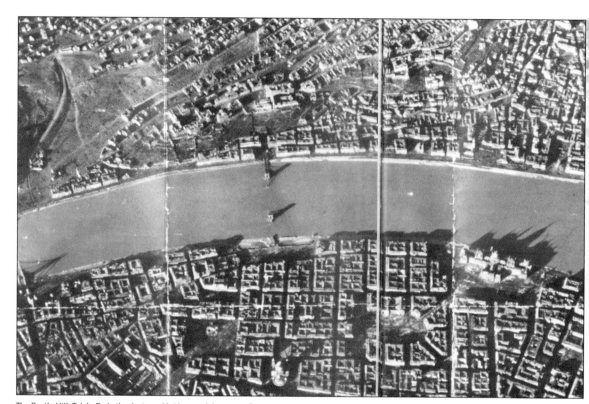

The Castle Hill, Tabán Park, the destroyed bridges and downtown Pest.

Városliget Park, Andrássy Avenue and the Eastern Railway Station.

Fortress Budapest | Photos

Aerial photo of Kálmán Tisza Square (today II. János Pál pápa Square), taken by an Il-2 of 451st Air Assault Regiment, 2.1.1945.

Aerial photo taken by an Il-2 of 91st Guards Air Assault Regiment at 500 metres on 2.1.1945.

AERIAL PHOTOS

Aerial photo of Angol Street, Lajos Kövér Street, Egressy Street and Szugló Street, taken by an Il-2 of the 92nd Guards Air Assault Regiment at 600 metres on 2.1.1945.

Aerial photo of the Eastern Rail Station, taken by an Il-2 of 809th Air Assault Regiment on 2.1.1945.

Aerial photo of Deák Square and Károly Boulevard, taken by an Il-2 of the 235th Air Assault Regiment on 14.1.1945.

Aerial photo of Süttő (ca. 50km northwest from Budapest), taken by an Il-2 of the 91st Guards Air Assault Regiment on 3.1.1945.

AERIAL PHOTOS

The results of the air attack by ten Il-2s (90th Guarsd Air Assault Regiment) at Gárdony on 22.1.1945.

The Vérmező and Széll Kálmán Square.

Fortress Budapest | Photos

Aerial photo of the Citadella and Gellért Hill.

THE BREAKOUT

Casualties of the breakout in Ostrom Street.

Casualties of the breakout on Széna Square.

Casulaties of the breakout in Szilágyi Erzsébet Alley.

Fallen defenders in front of a cellar.

THE BREAKOUT

Panzerbefehlswagen V Panther Ausf. G of 13. Panzer-Division destroyed at the end of of Retek Street.

Panzerbefehlswagen V Panther Ausf. G of 13. Panzer-Division destroyed at the end of of Retek Street.

Fortress Budapest | Photos

Destroyed Pz.Kpfw. V Panther Ausf. G of 13. Panzer-Division at the Retek Street - Dékán Street junction.

Destroyed Pz.Kpfw. V Panther Ausf. G of 13. Panzer-Division and the wreck of an Sd.Kfz.251/7 at the Retek Street - Dékán Street junction.

THE BREAKOUT

Destroyed Pz.Kpfw. V Panther Ausf. G of 13. Panzer-Division at the Retek Street - Dékán Street junction.

Destroyed Pz.Kpfw. V Panther Ausf. G of 13. Panzer-Division at the Retek Street - Dékán Street junction.

Destroyed Pz.Kpfw. V Panther Ausf. G of 13. Panzer-Division at the Retek Street - Dékán Street junction.

Knocked out Pz.IV70(V) in front of New Szent János Hospital. (This vehicle was later allocated trophy number 160 on Budafok-Háros.)

THE BREAKOUT

This German soldier fell during the breakout at Csillaghegy Station on the Szentendre commuter railway.

German POWs.

German and Hungarian POWs.

German and Hungarian POWs.

THE BREAKOUT

German and Hungarian POWs.

German and Hungarian POWs.

German and Hungarian POWs.

German and Hungarian POWs.

THE BREAKOUT

German and Hungarian POWs.

German and Hungarian POWs.

Dead soldiers on Széna Square, fallen during the breakout.

THE BREAKOUT

Dead German soldiers in the area of Nagykovácsi.

Dead German soldiers in the area of Nagykovácsi.

Dead German soldiers in the area of Nagykovácsi.

Assembly point for the soldiers of the Waffen-SS who succesfully broke out from Budapest.

BUDAPEST UNDER SIEGE

Soviet soldiers in a captured cross-country vehicle in Buda.

Wrecks on the edge of Vérmező.

The Kálvin Square and the Hungarian National Museum in the background.

Statue of Görgey Artúr on the Esztergom bastion, in front of the Military History Museum.

BUDAPEST UNDER SIEGE

The damaged buildings of the Royal Place and the Royal Barn.

The foreground of the Riding Hall.

Wrecks on the yard of the Royal Palace.

The yard of the Royal Palace.

BUDAPEST UNDER SIEGE

A villa on Bimbó Way.

The ruins of Krisztinaváros, seen from the Royal Palace.

The western (Buda) bridgehead of Erzsébet Bridge.

Ruined buildings in Csörsz Street.

BUDAPEST UNDER SIEGE

The southern side of the Citadelle.

The ruins of the Southern Railway Station. The T34/85 tank on the left side belonged to the 3rd Tank Brigade and was knocked out by the defenders on 30 January 1945.

The Károly Barracks (today Petőfi Barracks).

Wrecks of German SPWs on Horvát-kert.

BUDAPEST UNDER SIEGE

Wreck of a 4-cm Bofors anti-aircraft cannon at Horvát-kert.

Várfok Street after the breakout.

Fortress Budapest | Photos

Wrecks of DFS 230 gliders on Vérmező.

4-cm Bofors anti-aircraft cannon in the Royal Palace.

BUDAPEST UNDER SIEGE

Károly Boulevard and Deák Square with the Lutheran Church.

Nyugati Square

Fortress Budapest | Photos

FlaK 18 on Margit Boulevard at Mechwart Park.

Wrecks on Fortuna Street.

BUDAPEST UNDER SIEGE

The Margit Boulevard at Horvát Street.

The crossing at Krisztina Boulevard and Mészáros Street.

Artillery on Andrássy Street.

Corpses on Széll Kálmán Square after the breakout.

BUDAPEST UNDER SIEGE

Wrecked vehicles of Panzer-Divison "Feldherrnhalle" in Fényes Elek Street.

Dead SS-soldier on Margit Boulevard.

A destroyed house in Buda.

BUDAPEST UNDER SIEGE

Wrecks in Tabán Park.

Wrecks in downtown Buda.

The Habsburg-steps and the statue of Eugene Savoya in front of the Royal Palace.

Wrecks of wood-gas powered trucks in Buda.

BUDAPEST UNDER SIEGE

Wrecks in Roham Street.

The eastern gate of Alagút.

Burnt-out boxcar on Margit Boulevard.

Burnt-out boxcar on Margit Boulevard.

BUDAPEST UNDER SIEGE

This house was most probably hit by super-heavy artillery.

One of the buildings of the stronghold formed around the Centre of Agricultural Research.

The ruins of MTA Centre for Agricultural Research in Hermann Ottó street.

The ruins of MTA Centre for Agricultural Research.

BUDAPEST UNDER SIEGE

One of the buildings of the stronghold formed around the Centre of Agricultural Research.

Strengthened fire position of a strongpoint.

Ruins of the Barn of the Royal Palace.

Wrecks and dead horses in Döbrentei Street.

BUDAPEST UNDER SIEGE

An American made Soviet truck on the yard of the Royal Palace.

Armoured air-raid shelter at the Royal Palace.

BUDAPEST UNDER SIEGE

Wrecks on Szent György Square.

Steam-engines on the tracks of the tramway at the Southern Railway Station.

The Serbian Church in Tabán Park.

Wrecked vehicle of the 8. SS-Kavallerie-Division "Florian Geyer" in Margit Boulevard.

BUDAPEST UNDER SIEGE

The Széll Kálmán Square after the siege. Note the cyrillic letters on the road signs.

The ruins of the Ministry of Defence on Szent György Square.

Fortress Budapest | Photos

Wreck of a T-34/85 at the Southern Railway Station.

Wrecks at the southern end of Vérmező.

BUDAPEST UNDER SIEGE

DFS 230 glider slammed into the roof of Attila Street 35.

The remains of a PaK 43 heavy anti-tank gun on the northern side of the Citadelle.

The previous PaK 43 heavy anti-tank gun on the northern side of the Citadelle.

The Southern side of the Citadelle.

BUDAPEST UNDER SIEGE

Wrecks on the edge of Vérmező.

The Kapisztrán statue at the Military History Museum on Kapisztrán Square.

Ruined houses on Buda Hills.

Ruins on Castle Hill.

BUDAPEST UNDER SIEGE

Ruins of Sándor Palace.

The yard of the Royal Palace.

The yard of the Royal Palace.

The Royal Palace and Horvát Park.

BUDAPEST UNDER SIEGE

The ruins of Sándor-palace. and the Ministry of Defence.

A destroyed T-34/84 at the crossing of Kékgolyó Street and Ráth György Street.

BUDAPEST UNDER SIEGE

Wrecks next to Matthias Church.

MÁV Class 242 steam locomotive on the Southern Railway Station.

Destroyed factory building in Buda.

Anti-tank obstacles on Eskü Way (today Szabadsajtó Way).

BUDAPEST UNDER SIEGE

"Dragon's teeth" obstacles.

Dug in anti-tank obstacles made of rails

Dug in anti-tank obstacles made of rails

Dug in anti-tank obstacles made of rails

BUDAPEST UNDER SIEGE

The destroyed Széchenyi Chain Bridge.

The destroyed Széchenyi Chain Bridge.

The burning Hotel Ritz pictured from Buda.

"Dragon's teeth" obstacles on the bank of the Danube, on the Belgrád embankment.

BUDAPEST UNDER SIEGE

Bombed-out houses in Pest.

Bombed-out houses in Pest.

"Dragon's teeth" obstacles at the Pest bridgehead of Erzsébet Bridge on Kossuth Lajos Street.

Barricade made of wrecks on Türr István Street.

BUDAPEST UNDER SIEGE

Railcars on Rákosrendező railyard turned into a defence line.

Railcars on Rákosrendező railyard turned into a defence line.

Railcars on Rákosrendező railyard turned into a defence line.

Wreck of a FlaK 36/37 anti-aircraft gun.

BUDAPEST UNDER SIEGE

Railcars on Rákosrendező railyard turned into a defence line.

The Eastern Railway Station.

BUDAPEST UNDER SIEGE

Barricade in the downtown area of Pest

Budaörsi Street 26.

Budaörsi Street with the quarry of Gellért Hill.

Graves in front of Avar Street 2/A.

BUDAPEST UNDER SIEGE

The ruined building of Naphegy Street 1.

The ruined building of Naphegy Street 15.

BUDAPEST UNDER SIEGE

Grave of a German soldier in front of Lisznyai Street 15.

The view of Naphegy Square.

Gellérthegy Street 12-18 seen from Naphegy Street.

BUDAPEST UNDER SIEGE

The damaged buildings of the Hungarian Optical Works (MOM – Magyar Optikai Művek).

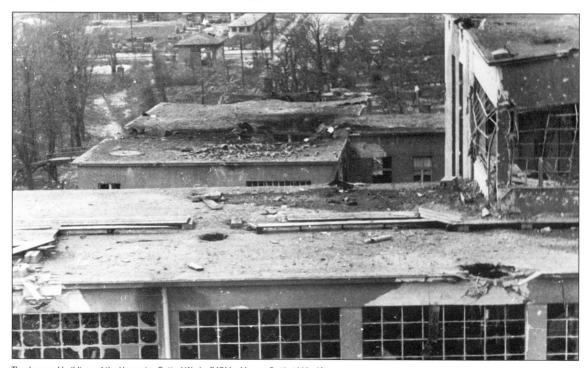

The damaged buildings of the Hungarian Optical Works (MOM – Magyar Optikai Művek).

Ruined buildings of Csörsz Street.

Ruined building on the corner of Csörsz Street and Böszörményi Street.

MILITARY EQUIPMENT

Captured artillery pieces in Soroksár.

Captured artillery pieces in Soroksár.

Captured artillery pieces in Soroksár.

Captured Panther Ausf. G in Korponay Street.

MILITARY EQUIPMENT

Captured Panther Ausf. G in Korponay Street.

Captured artillery pieces in Korponay Street.

Collected wrecks in Korponay street. There is an Italian-made Samovente 75/18 assault gun in the foreground.

Soviet troops inspect a knocked out Panther at the Dreher Brewery. The area was taken by the 297th Rifle Division on 4 January 1945.

MILITARY EQUIPMENT

Burnt-out Pz.IV/70(V) tank-hunter in Dobozi Street.

Burnt-out Pz.IV70(V) tank-hunter in Dobozi Street.

Burnt-out Pz.IV70(V) tank-hunter in Dobozi Street.

MILITARY EQUIPMENT

Abandoned PaK 40 anti-tank gun.

10,5-cm l.FH. 18 howitzer on József Boulevard.

Abandoned Pz.IV Ausf. J, probably in Városliget Park.

Abandoned Pz.IV Ausf. J, probably in Városliget Park.

MILITARY EQUIPMENT

Armoured train on Baross Square, in front of the Eastern Railway Station. The area was secured by Romanian troops on 15 January 1945.

Destroyed PaK 40 anti-tank gun on Nagykörút.

10,5-cm l.FH. 18 field howitzer on Teleki Square.

Destroyed Toldi light tank on Rákóczi Way.

MILITARY EQUIPMENT

Wrecks on József Nádor Square. There is a Toldi light tank in the foreground.

Panther Ausf. G of 13. Panzer-Division. The crew abandoned the vehicle after the failure of an attempted recovery, during the retreat from Pest.

The same Panther Ausf. G from a different angle.

The same Panther Ausf. G from a different angle.

MILITARY EQUIPMENT

The same Panther Ausf. G from a different angle.

The same Panther Ausf. G from a different angle.

4-cm Bofors anti-aircraft cannon in Váci Street, not far from the Panther seen in the previous pictures.

Hungarian 40M Turán tank.

MILITARY EQUIPMENT

Toldi light tank in a field repair shop in Pest.

Hungarian AFVs at the field repair shop in and around the Vígadó.

Hungarian Zrínyi II assault guns and 40M Turán tanks at the field repair shop in and around the Vígadó (concert hall).

4-cm Bofors anti-aircraft cannon on Deák Square.

MILITARY EQUIPMENT

Abandoned early production Bergepanther Ausf. D recovery vehicle.

Flak 36/37 anti-aircraft gun built on VOMAG bus chassis at the Fisherman's Bastion.

MILITARY EQUIPMENT

Flak 36/37 anti-aircraft gun built on VOMAG bus chassis on the Fisherman's Bastion.

Fortress Budapest | Photos

Flak 36/37 anti-aircraft gun built on VOMAG bus chassis at the Fisherman's Bastion.

MILITARY EQUIPMENT

Flak 36/37 anti-aircraft gun built on VOMAG bus chassis at the Fisherman's Bastion.

Fortress Budapest | Photos

Flak 36/37 anti-aircraft gun built on VOMAG bus chassis at the Fisherman's Bastion.

MILITARY EQUIPMENT

The wreck of a bus of the Royal Hungarian Post.

15-cm self-propelled infantry guns in Szalag Street. These vehicles later received trophy numbers 158 and 159 at Budafok-Háros.

Hungarian 10,5-cm field howitzers on Palota Way, in front of Fehérvári Gate.

Abandoned wrecks on Fő street. The Sd.Kfz. 250/9 light recon vehicle of 13. Panzer-Division can be seen on the right side of the picture.

MILITARY EQUIPMENT

Abandoned wrecks and Soviet trucks in front of Fő Street 10.

The remains of a FlaK 36/37 anti-aircraft gun in front of Fő Street 68.

Wreck of a FlaK 36/37 anti-aircraft gun in Fő Street at Imre Nagy Square.

MILITARY EQUIPMENT

Sd.Kfz. 231 heavy armoured car of 13. Panzer-Division and sd.Kfz. 251/21 "Drilling" armoured carriers in Fő Street, in front of the Capuchin Temple of Budapest.

Abandoned vehicles in Ponty Street.

Wrecks of an RSO and 2-cm anti-aircraft cannon in front of Fő Street 10.

The wreck of an Sd.Kfz. 251 armoured personnel carrier in front of Fő Street 12.

MILITARY EQUIPMENT

Wrecks on Fő Street at Szilágyi Dezső Square.

Wrecks on Fő Street at Szilágyi Dezső Square.

Wreck of a Jg.Pz. 38(t) "Hetzer" in front of Fő Street 81.

Nimród self-propelled anti-aircraft cannon in Irén Varsányi Street. There is a Botond cross-country truck in the background.

MILITARY EQUIPMENT

FlaK 36/37 anti-aircraft gun built on VOMAG bus chassis on Aranyhal Street.

FlaK 36/37 anti-aircraft gun built on VOMAG bus chassis on Aranyhal Street.

Damaged Nimród self-propelled anti-aircraft cannon at the corner of Fő Street and Csalogány Street. There is the remains of a Csaba armoured car in the background.

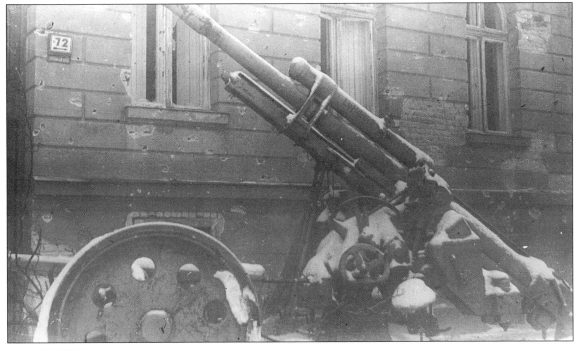
Captured FlaK M31 (r) anti-aircraft gun.

MILITARY EQUIPMENT

Sd.Kfz. 231 heavy armoured car of 13. Panzer-Division on the Bem embankment.

Wrecks on Szilágyi Dezső Square.

Fortress Budapest | Photos

Wrecks on Szilágyi Dezső Square.

FlaK 36/37 anti-aircraft guns on railcars at Szilágyi Dezső Square.

MILITARY EQUIPMENT

15-cm "Grille" self-propelled infantry gun of 13. Panzer-Division in Lánchíd Street, at the Ybl Miklós Square.

Wrecks on Margit Boulevard in front of the destroyed Regent-house.

The remains of a FlaK 36/37 anti-aircraft gun in a street of Buda.

Italian-made M15/40 light tank in Perc Street.

MILITARY EQUIPMENT

Italian-made M15/40 light tank in Nagyszombat Street.

The wreck of Pz.Beob.Wg. III of Panzer-Division "Feldherrnhalle" in Tigris Street.

Fortress Budapest | Photos

The wreck of Pz.Beob.Wg. III of Panzer-Division "Feldherrnhalle" in Tigris Street.

MILITARY EQUIPMENT

Destroyed T-34/85 of 21st Guards Tank Brigade, 5th Guards Tank Corps at the corner of Ibrahim Street and Karolina Way. It was destroyed by a Hungarian-made "shooting-mine".

Destroyed T-34/85 of 21st Guards Tank Brigade, 5th Guards Tank Corps at the corner of Ibrahim Street and Karolina Way. It was destroyed by a Hungarian-made "shooting-mine".

Remains of a 15-cm "Hummel self-propelled howitzer in Fehérvári Way.

Wreck of a Zrínyi II assault gun in Budaörsi way.

MILITARY EQUIPMENT

Half-ready hulls of Zrínyi II assault guns.

Wreck of Csaba armoured car in Pasaréti Way.

Wrecks in Mészöly Street, opposite Hadik Barracks.

MILITARY EQUIPMENT

FlaK 36/37 anti-aircraft gun and Sd.Kfz. 9 FAMO towing vehicle in front of Attila Street 79.

Stripped skeletons of DFS 230 gliders and other wrecks at the edge of Vérmező.

Wreck of an Sd.Kfz. 231 heavy armoured car of 13. Panzer-Division at the southern edge of Vérmező. Mikó Street can be seen in the background.

Sd.Kfz. 222 light armoured car, also from 13. Panzer-Divison at the same place.

MILITARY EQUIPMENT

Wrecks of vehicles at the southern edge of Vérmező.

Wrecks of vehicles at the southern edge of Vérmező.

Fortress Budapest | Photos

Wrecks of vehicles at the southern edge of Vérmező.

MILITARY EQUIPMENT

Pz.Kpfw. V Panther Ausf. G of 13. Panzer-Division in Krisztina Boulevard, next to Vérmező.

Wrecks of a Bergepanther, and Sd.Kfz. 251 armoured personnel carrier and the same Panther in Krisztina Boulevard.

Remains of a FlaK 36/37 and various wrecks at the edge of Vármező.

The remains of an Sd.Kfz. 251 personnel carrier and a 10.5-cm "Wespe" self-propelled howitzer (or its ammunition carrier version) in Krisztina Boulevard, next to Vérmező.

MILITARY EQUIPMENT

Closer look of the same vehicle of the previous picture. The white number on the side plate designates a Soviet unit (not a trophy number!)

Destroyed T-34/85, probably from 2nd Guards Mechanized Corps.

Wrecks of German vehicles in Krisztina Boulevard, next to Vérmező.

Wreck of an Sd.Kfz. 251 armoured personnel carrier in Krisztina Boulevard.

MILITARY EQUIPMENT

Zrínyi II assault gun of First Lieutenant Tibor Rátz in Krisztina Boulevard, at the Northern tip of the Southern Railway Station.

Zrínyi II assault gun of First Lieutenant Tibor Rátz in Krisztina Boulevard, at the northern tip of the Southern Railway Station.

Zrínyi II assault gun of First Lieutenant Tibor Rátz in Krisztina Boulevard, at the northern tip of the Southern Railway Station.

Zrínyi II assault gun of First Lieutenant Tibor Rátz in Krisztina Boulevard, at the northern tip of the Southern Railway Station.

MILITARY EQUIPMENT

Soviet fighting vehicles, captured on the Eastern Front which were put on exhibition at the northern tip of Vérmező.

Wreck of a Soviet BA-10 armoured car, captured on the Eastern Front which was put on exhibition at the Northern tip of Vérmező.

German and Hungarian artillery pieces on Vérmező. Also there is a Csaba armoured car in the background (on the right side of the picture).

Artillery pieces on Vérmező and the exhibited vehicles in the background.

MILITARY EQUIPMENT

Artillery pieces at the northern edge of Vérmező, in front of Attila Way 133.

Wrecks of German vehicles and a Soviet T-34/85 (most probably from the 3rd Tank Brigade) at the Krisztina Boulevard - Vérmező Way crossing.

Fortress Budapest | Photos

Sd.Kfz. 251/1 Ausf C of the 13. Panzer-Division and an Sd.Kfz. 11 half-track on Dózsa György Square.

Front view of the Sd.Kfz. 251/1 Ausf. C seen in the previous photo.

MILITARY EQUIPMENT

Wrecks on Dózsa György Square.

Wrecks on Dózsa György Square.

Fortress Budapest | Photos

Wreck of a 15-cm "Hummel" self-propelled howitzer of Panzer-Division "Feldherrnhalle" in Kriszitna Boulevard, roughly at Attila Way 15.

Wreck of a 15-cm "Hummel" self-propelld howitzer of Panzer-Division "Feldherrnhalle" in Kriszitna Boulevard, roughly at Attila Way 15.

MILITARY EQUIPMENT

Wreck of a 15-cm "Hummel" self-propelled howitzer of Panzer-Division "Feldherrnhalle" in Kriszitna Boulevard, roughly at Attila Way 15.

Wreck of a 15-cm "Hummel" self-propelled howitzer of Panzer-Division "Feldherrnhalle" in Kriszitna Boulevard, roughly at Attila Way 15.

The remains of a Beobachtungspanzer III in front of Attila Way 17.

The remains of a Beobachtungspanzer III in front of Attila Way 17.

MILITARY EQUIPMENT

15-cm "Hummel" self-propelled howitzers southeast of Bethlen udvar. The front vehicle is trophy number 115 (later 141).

15-cm "Hummel" self-propelled howitzer in front of Saint Catherine Church.

A couple of abandoned 15-cm "Hummel" self-propelled howitzers captured in working order by Soviet troops in Apród Street.

A couple of abandoned 15-cm "Hummel" self-propelled howitzers captured in working order by Soviet troops in Apród Street.

MILITARY EQUIPMENT

A couple of abandoned 15-cm "Hummel" self-propelled howitzers captured in working order by Soviet troops in Apród Street.

A couple of abandoned 15-cm "Hummel" self-propelled howitzers captured in working order by Soviet troops in Apród Street.

Hungarian Zrínyi II assault gun in Apród Street.

The same Zrínyi II and a 15-cm "Hummel" self-propelled howitzer.

MILITARY EQUIPMENT

15-cm "Hummel" self-propelled howitzer of the Panzer-Division "Feldherrnhalle" next to the Serbian Church.

15-cm "Hummel" self-propelled howitzer of the Panzer-Division "Feldherrnhalle" next to the Serbian Church.

15-cm "Hummel" self-propelled howitzer next to Saint Catherine Church.

The 15-cm "Hummel" self-propelled howitzer next to Saint Catherine Church looks operational.

MILITARY EQUIPMENT

This 15-cm "Hummel" self-propelled howitzer next to the Serbian Church seems functional.

German fighting vehicles that are considered functional or at least repairable next to the Serbian Church.

German fighting vehicles that are considered functional or at least repairable next to the Serbian Church.

One of the 15-cm Hummels seen in the previous picture.

MILITARY EQUIPMENT

The Serbian Church and Saint Catherine Church.

Destroyed Pz.Kpfw. IV Ausf. J.

15-cm "Hummel" self-propelled howitzer in Buda.

Wreck of 38M RÁBA Botond cross-country truck.

MILITARY EQUIPMENT

German truck abandoned at Vígszínház.

Artillery pieces at a collecting point.

Abandoned 15-cm heavy infantry gun (s.I.G. 33)

MILITARY EQUIPMENT

Overturned truck of I./Pz.Gr.Rgt. 93 (13. Panzer-Division). There is a "supply bomb" on its platform.

Abandoned German cross-country vehicles.

Abandoned Jg.Pz. 38(t) "Hetzer" tank-hunter in the area of the stronghold constructed in Hermann Ottó Way.

MILITARY EQUIPMENT

Wrecks of trucks and towing vehicles at a collecting point.

Soviet T-34/85 towing a couple of captured German FAMO half-tracks at the foot of Gellért Hill.

Pz.Kpfw. IV Ausf. J next to the embankment in Kelenföld.

Pz.Kpfw. IV Ausf. J in Bartók Béla Way.

MILITARY EQUIPMENT

Pz.Kpfw. IV Ausf. J in Fehérvári Way. The building in the background is Náday Ferenc Street 7.

Pz.Kpfw. IV Ausf. J in Fehérvári Way. The building in the background is Náday Ferenc Street 7.

Flakpanzer IV "Möbelwagen" probably at the crossing of Alkotás Street and Csörsz Street.

Pz.IV70(V) tank-hunter, probably at Csörsz Street.

MILITARY EQUIPMENT

Zrínyi II assault gun on Kelenföld.

Two Bergepanthers in Budaörsi Way (today BAH junction). The Bergepanther with trophy number 120 was captured outside of Budapest.

Pz.Kpfw. V Panther Ausf. G on Alkotás Way (at that time Gömbös Gyula Way)

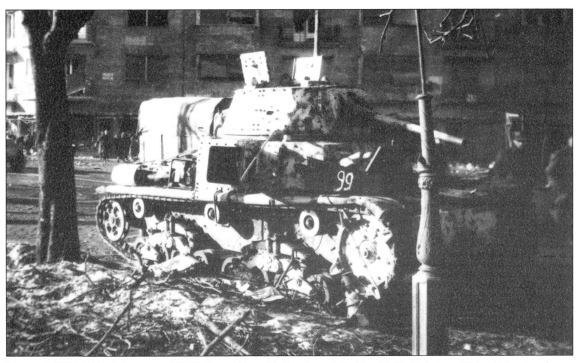
Italian-made M15/42 light tank at the corner of Alkotás Way and Magyar Jakobinus Square (at that time Gömbös Gyula Way and Endresz György Square).

MILITARY EQUIPMENT

Italian-made M15/42 light tank at the corner of Alkotás Way and Márvány Street.

Pz.Kpfw. V Panther Ausf. G in Alkotás Way.

StuG. III assault gun at the Attila Way - Alagút Street crossing.

Pz.IV70(V) at the corner of Alagút Street and Pauler Street.

MILITARY EQUIPMENT

Pz.Kpfw. V Panther Ausf. G in Városmajor Street.

StuG. III Ausf. G of Panzer-Division "Feldherrnhalle" in Maros Street.

Pz.Kpfw. V Panther Ausf. A at the Alagút Street - Krisztina Boulevard crossing.

Pz.Kpfw. V Panther Ausf. A and Ausf. G at the Alagút Street - Krisztina Boulevard crossing.

MILITARY EQUIPMENT

Pz.IV70(V) at the corner of Alagút Street and Pauler Street.

Pz.Kpfw. V Panther Ausf. A at the Alagút Street - Krisztina Boulevard crossing.

Pz.IV70(A) of the 13. Panzer-Division in front of Krisztina Boulevard 71.

Pz.IV70(A) of 13. Panzer-Division in front of Krisztina Boulevard 71.

MILITARY EQUIPMENT

Pz.Kpfw. V Panther Ausf. A and Ausf. G at the Alagút Street - Krisztina Boulevard crossing.

Pz.Kpfw. V Panther Ausf. A at the Alagút Street - Krisztina Boulevard crossing.

Pz.Kpfw. V Panther Ausf. G (rebuilt with early turret) in Krisztina Boulevard.

Pz.Kpfw. V Panther Ausf. G (rebuilt with early turret) in Krisztina Boulevard.

MILITARY EQUIPMENT

Pz.IV70(A) of the 13. Panzer-Division in front of Krisztina Boulevard 71.

Pz.IV70(V) in Krisztina Boulevard.

Bergepanther Ausf. D in Krisztina Boulevard.

MILITARY EQUIPMENT

Pz.Kpfw. V Panther Ausf. G (rebuilt with early turret) in Krisztina Boulevard.

10,5-cm self-propelled guns "Wespe" (or its ammo-carrier version) of Panzer-Division "Feldherrnhalle" in Krisztina Boulevard. The vehicle with trophy number 121 was captured outside of Budapest.

Flakpanzer IV Möbelwagen in Attila Way.

MILITARY EQUIPMENT

Bergepanther Ausf. D in Krisztina Boulevard. (This vehicle had trophy number 145 at the Budafok-Háros collecting point later.)

15-cm "Hummel" self-propelled gun in front of Attila Street 23.

15-cm "Hummel" self-propelled gun at the southeastern side of Bethlen-udvar. This vehicle later received trophy number 141 at Budafok-Háros.

MILITARY EQUIPMENT

Wreck of a 15-cm Hummel self-propelled gun and a Sd.Kfz.251/21 "Drilling" delete space in Attila Way.

The same location from a different view.

There are three Sd.Kfz. 252/21 "Drilling" and a Soviet T-28 tank in the row beside the wreck of a 15-cm "Hummel" self-propelled howitzer, trophy number 141 (earlier it was trophy 115).

MILITARY EQUIPMENT

41M Turán tank.

Sd.Kfz. 251/9 assault personnel carrier of 13. Panzer-Division, and a "Drilling" behind it without armament.

10,5-cm "Wespe" self-propelled howitzer. According to original data there was only one "Wespe" inside the city during the siege, which belonged to the Panzer-Division "Feldherrnhalle".

40M and 41M Turán tanks.

MILITARY EQUIPMENT

41M Turán tank and a 15-cm heavy field howitzer. The wooden cover was to protect the gun recuperator from shrapnel damage.

This Bergepanther wore trophy number 109 earlier, when it was photographed on Krisztina Boulevard.

Pz.Kpfw. II Ausf. F light tank, probably from 239. Assault Artillery Brigade.

15-cm "Grille" self-propelled infantry gun of the 13. Panzer-Division, which was captured in Szalag Street by Soviet troops.

MILITARY EQUIPMENT

Toldi light tank.

40M Turán with side skirts, but without armament.

Panzerbefehlswagen (command) III of 13. Panzer-Division, with turret number "R01".

StuG. III Ausf. G and a Hungarian Zrínyi II assault howitzer.

MILITARY EQUIPMENT

40M Turán tank.

This Pz.IV70(V) was knocked out at the New Saint John Hospital, probably during the breakout.

41M Turán tank with side skirts.

Early Bergepanther Ausf. D, which probably wasn't caprured in Budapest.

MILITARY EQUIPMENT

The Italian-made M15/42 light tank in the background belonged to the 12. Polizei-Panzer-Kompanie, but nothing is known about the origin of the Matilda standing in front of it.

41M Turán tank.

Wrecks were transported to Budafok-Háros not only from the capital itself, but from the area west of Budapest too.

Wrecks were transported to Budafok-Háros not only from the capital itself, but from the area west of Budapest too.

COMMAND CENTRE ON SAS-HEGY HILL

Tunnel contact to the Danube.

Waterpump station.

The entrance of the headquarters on Sas-hegy Hill.

Reinforced concrete bunkers in the area of the HQ.

COMMAND CENTRE ON SAS-HEGY HILL

Reinforced concrete bunkers in the area of the HQ.

An air gauge above the command centre.

A small building above the command centre.

Air-defence centre of the Hungarian air space.

Mechanical elements of the command centre.

COMMAND CENTRE ON SAS-HEGY HILL

Air filter equipment.

Boiler.

Telephone centre.

Reinforced concrete fire-control bunker.

THE SOVIET DANUBE FLOTILLA AND THE AIR FORCES

Boat of the Danube Flotilla.

Boats of the Danube Flotilla.

Boats of the Danube Flotilla.

Boat of the Danube Flotilla.

THE SOVIET DANUBE FLOTILLA AND THE AIR FORCES

Boat of the Danube Flotilla.

Boat of the Danube Flotilla.

Ju 52 transport plane.

THE SOVIET DANUBE FLOTILLA AND THE AIR FORCES

He 111 of KG 4.

He 111 of KG 4.

Remains of DFS 230 gliders on Vérmező.

Remains of DFS 230 glider on Vérmező.

THE SOVIET DANUBE FLOTILLA AND THE AIR FORCES

Crashed Ju 52.

Briefing on the tail of an Il-2 assault plane.

Briefing before a mission over Budapest.

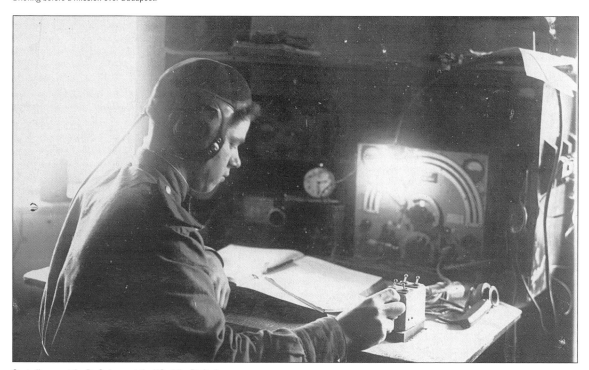
Controll room of the Po-2 planes at the HQ of the 5th Air Army.

PERSONS

Marshal Rodion Malinovsky, commander of the 2nd Ukrainian Front.

Marshal Fyodor Tolbukhin, commander of the 3rd Ukrainian Front.

Colonel-General Matvei Zakharov, the chief of staff of 2nd Ukrainian Front.

Colonel-General Goryunov, the commander of 5th Air Army.

Rear-Admiral Kholostyakov, the commander of the Danube Flotilla.

Colonel-General Shumilov, the commander of 7th Guards Army.

Colonel-General Trofimenko, the commander of 27th Army.

General Zhmachenko, the commander of 40th Army.

PERSONS

Major-General Kolchuk, the commander of 46th Army.

Lieutenant-General Gorshkov, the commander of the cavalry-mechanized group of the same name.

Lieutenant-General Pliev, the commander of the cavalry-mechanized group of the same name.

Major-General Saveliev, the commander of 5th Guards Tank Corps.

Lieutenant-General Akhmanov, the commander of 23rd Tank Corps.

Lieutenant-General Volkov, the commander of 9th Guards Mechanized Corps.

Major-General Golovskoy, the commander of 4th Guards Cavalry Corps.

Lieutenant-General Sokolov, the commander of 6th Guards Cavalry Corps.

PERSONS

General Rubanyuk, the commander of 10th Guards Rifle Corps.

Major-General Afonin, the commander of 18th Guards Rifle Corps.

Major-General Sosedov, acting commander of 18th Guards Rifle Corps and chief of staff of the Budapest Group.

Major-General Grigorovich, the commander of 23rd Rifle Corps.

Major-General Lazko, the commander of 30th Rifle Corps.

Major-General Sviridov, the commander of 37th Rifle Corps.

Major-General Akimenko, the commander of 75th Rifle Corps.

Mikhail Ashik, Hero of the Soviet Union and platoon commander with 144th Battalion of 83rd Naval Infantry Brigade.

PERSONS

Major-General Frolov (right), the commander of 66th Guards Rifle Division, in his HQ in Pest, early January 1945

SS-Obergruppenführer Karl Pfeffer-Wildebruch, commander of IX. SS Mountain Corps.

Gerhard Schmidhuber (Major General), commander of the 13. Panzer-Division..

Fortress Budapest | Photos

Iván Hindy (Lieutenant General) commander of the Hungarian 1. Army Corps.

Ernő Csipkés (Colonel, Major General) commander of Budapest.

Ernő Billnitzer (Lieutenant General) commander of the Assault Artillery Group named after him.

Oszkár Variházy (Lieutenant Colonel), commander of the Hungarian 10. Infantry Division, then commander of Budai Önkéntes Zászlóalj (Buda Voluntary Battalion from 12 February 1945 - Regiment from 15 February 1945).

PERSONS

General der Panzertruppe Hermann Balck, commander of the German 6. Armee

Joachim Ruhmor (SS-Brigadeführer), commander of 8. SS-Cavalry-Division "Florian Geyer".

August Zehender (SS-Brigadeführer), commander of 22nd SS-Cavalry-Division.

Wilhelm Schöning (Lieutenant Colonel reserve), commander of Panzer-Grenadier-Regiment 66.

FORTRESS BUDAPEST
LEAFLETS

LEAFLETS

Leaflet for the German defenders of the besieged Budapest

Nachrichten
für die
deutschen Truppen

1. Aus dem Kessel Gross-Budapest

Der Feind hat die Absicht, den Brückenkopf ostwärts der Donau in letzter Minute vor Eintreffen des deutschen Entsatzes zu zerschlagen, Wieder hatte der Gegner zahlenmässig weit überlegene Infanteriekräfte, Panzer und Schlachtflieger eingesetzt. Das wütende Artlleriefeuer setzte kaum einen Augenblick aus. Die tapfere Besatzung hielt diesen Angriffen im Wesentlichen stand. Wo einzelne Strassenzüge aufgegeben wurden, geschah es unter schwersten Verlusten für den Feind. Zwei „T 34". 7 Pak, wurden vernichtet, weitere Waffen erbeutet. 59 Gefangene wurden eingebracht.

2. Das Oberkommando
der Wehrmacht gibt bekannt

Berlin, 5. Januar.

Die Schlacht in den nördlichen Ardennen hat sich gestern gesteigert. Im zusammengefassten Feuer aller Waffen fasten sich erneut zum Durchbruch ansetzenden amerikanischen Divisionen so nach geringen Anfangserfolgen wieder fest. Im Raum von Bast halten unsere Panzerverbände ihren starken Druck aufrecht. F che Angriffe scheiterten.

Die Front zwischen Saargemünd und dem Rhein ist in Bewegung. Trotz der Gegenangriffe der inzwischen herangeführten sind chen Verbände sind unsere Truppen besonders in den unteren Vogesen weiter im Vordringen. Neben zahlreichen Orten in Lothringen wu die Stadt Weissenburg im Elsass vom Feinde befreit, die Lauter na Süden überschritten. 76 Panzer und Panzerfahrzeuge wurden geste im Westen erbeutet oder vernichtet, auch zahlreiche Geschütze und Kriegsgerät aller Art fielen in unsere Hand. In Mittelitalien dauern die schweren Abwehrkämpfe an. Im Raum nördlich Faenza behaupten unsere Truppen das Feld gegen die feindlichen Durchbruchsve che. Nordwestlich Ravenna stehen sie in schweren Kämpfen gegen gestossene feindliche Verbände.

Die Schlacht um Budapest geht weiter. Die deuts rischen Verteidiger schlugen auch gestern starke fein am Ostrand der Stadt zurück. Um einzelne Einbruch erb tter gekämpft.

Den zwischen dem Garam und Rim szo schewisten blieben nenneeswerte Erfolge sche Kampfgruppe, die in unsere Stellun im Gegenangriff durch. unsere Panz

159

Starke Verbände deutscher Schlachtflieger unterstützten auch gestern die Kämpfe des Heeres in Ungarn und setzten 18 Panzer ausser Gefecht. Dreissig sowjetische Flugzeuge wurden vernichtet, davon 26 in Luftkämpfen durch unsere Jäger und Schlachtflieger. In Kurland scheiterten südlich Frauenburg mehrere örtliche Angriffe der Bolsc̓ ten.

Am gestrigen Tage waren über dem Reichsgebiete nur kleinere Verbände feindlicher Tiefflieger. In den Abendstunden und um Mitternacht griffen schnelle britische Kampfflugzeuge erneut die Reichshauptstadt an.

Das Feuer unserer Vergeltungswaffen auf London wurde verstärkt.

3. Kurznachrichten

Vom ungarischen Kriegsschauplatz:

Zwischen dem Ostufer des Balaton und dem Südufer der Donau hat sich die Wucht der Kämpfe erheblich gesteigert. Westlich Stuhlweissenburg und nördlich Mór wurden mehrere sowjetische Angriffe abgewiesen. In dem Raum nordostwärts Felsögalla mussten die Bolschewisten schwere Schläge einstecken. In tagelangem Ringen haben starke deutsche Verbände von Panzerkampftruppen und Formationen der Luftwaffe unterstützt die Absicht der sowjetischen Führung, aus dem Vértes-Gebirge herauszutreten und auf Komárom durchzustossen, vereitelt und mehrere Regimenter im Gegenangriff völlig vernichtet. Die Artilleriestellungen des Gegners wurden überrollt und zahlreiche Stellungen genommen verbessert ... bolschewistische Reserven, die in Gewaltmärschen heraneilten, wurden noch in der Entwicklung zusammengeschlagen und dabei weitere 59 Kampfwagen zerstört. Die Menschen und Materialverluste der Sowjets sind ausserordentlich hoch. Die Besatzung der ungarischen Hauptstadt wehrte alle Angriffe von Osten her ab und eroberte in heftigen Gegenangriffen mehrere Strassenblocks zurück.

Beatus Ille!

Warten ist die bittere Pille
Budapester Zivadille.
Beiderseits der Donaurille
hält der Russe uns in der Hülle
In erwartungsvoller Stille
warten wir auf Gen'ral Gille.
Gille, komm mach kille kille
hau dem Russen auf die Brille,
dass er mit des Blitzes Schnille
leuchtet von Budapestens Schwille:
komm mit Dröhnen dumpf und schrille
... Graus und Grille,
... bei Mut und Wille:
... mach Kille — Kille!

LEAFLETS

Soviet leaflet for the Hungarian defenders of Budapest in the war diary of 311st Guards Rifle Regiment

...ий ...ей теплый Грачев — 7 стрелков, взвод сапер.
Всего — 39 активных штыков.

На вооружении штурмовой группы — 3 ручных
пулемета, две 45 мм пушки, два 82 мм миномета,
один станковый пулемет, ружье ПТР, 3 автомата,
120 ручных гранат.

В целях улучшения своего оборонительного
рубежа, 311 гв.сп с 13.00 вел бой за овладение
домов в кв. 1914. В результате заняли два сильно
укрепленных дома на с.з. скатах высоты 259.0.

С НП ведется непрерывное наблюдение за пр-ком.
Замечается большое передвижение немецкой пехоты
и автомашин в северном направлении Будапешт.

14 января.

На боевом участке группы противник силою
до 25 человек пытался захватить два дома,
заняли нами 12 января.
Потеряв половину личного состава, немцы отошли.
КП полка — уг. Бела-Кирай.

15—16 января.

311 гв.сп оборудует свой район обороны
инженерными сооружениями.

Зенитчики подбили одно "юнкерса", пытав-
шегося сбросить на парашюте боепитание

LEAFLETS

Soviet leaflet for the German defenders of Buda, which would also serve as a pass to those who voluntarily surrendered

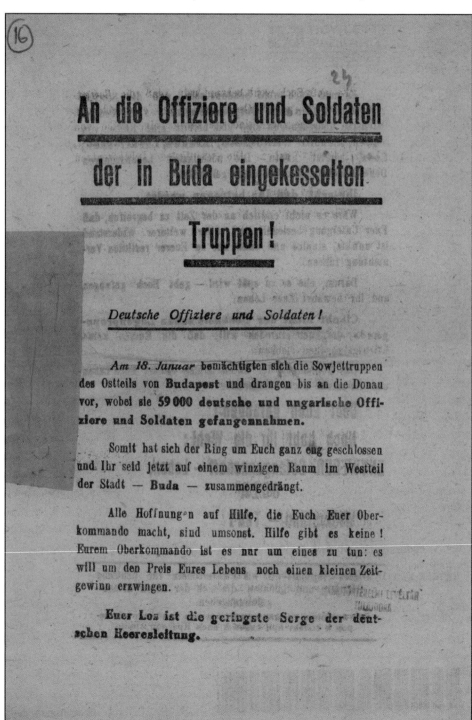

Es muß Euch wohl bekannt sein, daß die Sowjet-truppen in **Polen** und **Ostpreußen** zur entscheidenden Offensive übergegangen sind und bereits eine Reihe von Städten, darunter **WARSCHAU**, Krakau, Czenstochau, Lodz, besetzt haben. Die wichtigsten Lebenszentren Deutschlands sind unmittelbar gefährdet.

Ihr seht, daß Ihr betrogen werdet.

Wäre es nicht endlich an der Zeit zu begreifen, daß Euer Untergang besiegelt ist? Aller weiterer Widerstand ist unnütz, sinnlos und kann nur zu Euerer restlosen Ver-nichtung führen.

Darum, ehe es zu spät wird — gebt Euch gefangen und Ihr bewahrt Euer Leben.

Glaubt nicht der Goebbels'schen Lügenpropa-ganda, die Euch einreden will, daß die Russen keine Kriegsgefangenen machen.

Das Kommando der Roten Armee sichert Euch Leben und Heimkehr nach Kriegsende.

Gebt Euch gefangen!
Noch habt Ihr die Wahl:
ENTWEDER Gefangenschaft — Leben,
ODER
Widerstand — Tod!

Dieses Flugblatt gilt als Passierschein für deutsche Offiziere und Soldaten, die sich der Roten Armee gefangengeben.

Эта листовка служит пропуском для немецких офице-ров и солдат при сдаче в плен Красной Армии.